C000015891

ABOUT THE AUTHOR

Dr Jo Murphy-Lawless is a sociologist who has published widely in two fields: on issues of poverty and social exclusion and on the social and medical aspects of women's childbearing in both the Irish and international contexts. In the 1960s, she set up the Dublin Tutorial Programme, an out-of-school support project for children from the Sheriff Street area in the north inner city. She worked in Sean MacDermott Street from 1982 to 1984, during the first wave of widespread heroin use, with a young people's youth services group. From 1985 onwards, she has carried out a number of commissioned studies on illegal drug use and the social aspects of HIV and AIDS.

FIGHTING BACK

Women and the Impact of Drug Abuse on Families and Communities

Jo Murphy-Lawless

The Liffey Press
Dublin

Published by
The Liffey Press
307 Clontarf Road
Dublin 3, Ireland
www.theliffeypress.com

© 2002 Jo Murphy-Lawless

A catalogue record of this book is
available from the British Library.

ISBN 1-904148-09-3

All rights reserved. No part of this publication may be reproduced
or transmitted in any form or by any means, including
photocopying and recording, without written permission of the
publisher. Such written permission must also be obtained before
any part of this publication is stored in a retrieval system of any
nature. Requests for permission should be directed to
The Liffey Press, 307 Clontarf Road, Dublin 3, Ireland.

Printed in the Republic of Ireland by Colour Books Ltd.

CONTENTS

ACKNOWLEDGEMENTS

The research project which forms the basis for this book was made possible by the generosity of the following funders: the Joseph Rowntree Charitable Trust, the Katherine Howard Foundation, the Combat Poverty Agency, the Eastern Regional Health Authority, Glaxo-Wellcome (Ireland), the Bank of Ireland and the Trinity Trust. I want to thank them for the confidence they expressed in funding the project from the outset. Stephen Pittam, Philip Jacob, Patricia Kennedy, Brenda Enright, Dominick Jenkins, Helen Johnston, Noelle Spring, Oisín Murphy-Lawless, Dara Higgins, Julie Cruikshank, Mel Macgiobúin and David Silke gave vital encouragement and practical support, for which I am especially grateful. Clare Brady, Emer Coveney, Anne Davis, Passerose Mantoy, Kathleen Murray and Sheila Sheridan contributed invaluable assistance with fieldwork, background reports and transcription of data. The publication of the research was made possible through the generosity of the Joseph Rowntree Charitable Trust and the Katherine Howard Foundation.

Many people gave the research project their time and consideration. They deserve great thanks for their commitment. Above all, there was a core group of women who permitted their lives and work to be intruded on for the fieldwork and interviews. Because it has been essential to preserve complete confidentiality, it is not possible to name them. But they have my heartfelt thanks for agreeing to that intrusion. My hope is that the book can bring their perspectives and analyses one step further along in the search for a more participatory process for women and their families in building the social and economic future of the local communities in Dublin's north inner city. A summary of the research is available as a separate short document from the North Inner City Drugs Task Force.

Chapter One

THE NORTH INNER CITY:
THREE DECADES OF MARGINALISATION

THE HEROIN CRISIS

The north inner city of Dublin has been living with the "heroin epidemic" since the end of the 1970s and the local communities which have borne its damage have experienced fundamental change. Some elements of that change were already in progress before heroin arrived. At the beginning of the 1970s, the decline in traditional industries introduced the realities of long-term unemployment, especially for adult men. This experience went on for far too long, affecting those who were already adult workers at that time, their children who were growing up into a climate of no available work and in turn their grandchildren as well. Thus, three generations were affected by industrial decline. Widespread heroin addiction, coming on top of this, imposed another series of painful realities for individuals, families and communities, which forced a readjustment of almost every aspect of everyday life, from the safety of play facilities for small children to the breakdown of family relationships.

Heroin has also had a major economic impact on these communities. In areas where there was an increasingly strong statistical likelihood of being unemployed, drug trading and drug dealing came to have a major influence on the local economy. Drug dealing represented huge sources of revenue for the large-scale dealers and, for many heroin users, a necessary activity to help them pay for their addiction. In 1993–94, it was conservatively estimated that the annual circulation of money which made up the hard drugs economy in the north-east inner city (covering six parish

boundaries) was £9.1 million (ICON,[1] 1994, pp. 72–73). That estimate was the result of a micro-study, based on the street cost of
heroin at the time, taking into account drug usage patterns of clients registered with local clinics and needle exchange services.

The number of drug users entering treatment for the first time
in the greater Dublin area as a whole rose from 624 in 1990 to
1,396 by 1995, with 77 per cent of those being primarily opiate users (O'Brien and Moran, 1997). There were approximately 200
drug users in treatment from the ten wards in the north inner city
in 1993 (O'Higgins and O'Brien, 1994). By 1996, this had risen to
642,[2] as recorded by the National Drug Reporting System (Moran,
O'Brien and Duff, 1997, p. 34). Concentrating just on the postal
district of Dublin 1, and adjusting for double-counting through an
attributor code, the sister study to this current work found in 1997
that there were 477 people who were heroin users, 91 per cent of
those being in treatment agencies (Coveney, et al., 1999). This was
acknowledged to be a clear underestimate of the real prevalence
rates (ibid.); however, the study data enabled the authors to pos-
tulate an incidence of heroin addiction of 20.44 users per 1,000 of
the population (ibid.), compared with a figure for the greater Dublin area of 3.6 per 1,000 of the population for 1995 (O'Higgins and
Duff, 1997). The latest figures from the National Drug Treatment
Reporting System indicate that, for 1998, there were 687 opiate
users registered for treatment in the North Inner City Electoral
Borough (personal communication, Mary O'Brien, NDTRS, Drug
Misuse Research Division, Health Research Board).

It has been extremely difficult for researchers to emerge with
even this level of quantitative information. There are very complex
problems of methodology in trying to calculate possible rates of
drug use prevalence because of the types of data available, how
accurately it is recorded, and whether that data is actually usable,
let alone the associated problems of statistical analysis. Irish re-

---

[1] ICON is a network of community groups in the northeast inner city which was
established in 1993 and which had, at that time, a specific drugs focus through its
Inter-Agency Drugs Project. See also Chapter Seven.

[2] These were contacts as distinct from persons, as there were no attributor codes
in use by the system at that time, which would have helped to eliminate double-
counting.

searchers are working towards meeting the standards recommended by the European Monitoring Centre for Drugs and Drug Addiction in estimating prevalence, but there is some distance to go before prevalence estimates can be used on a comparative basis with real confidence.

Whatever about these methodological problems, the impact of heroin use on everyday life is such that responding to it remains an urgent priority for the state and for the community, one that the recent ICON Action Plan states "demands flexible responses at local level because of its huge complexities" (ICON, 1999). ICON refers to the problems that it has experienced in trying, as a core grouping in the community sector in the north inner city, to generate sufficient levels of response (both long-term and short-term) to drugs. This has exhausted its resources,which in turn has "had a negative impact on the unity of groups under its umbrella" (ibid., p. 15). Both ICON and the CityWide Drugs Crisis Campaign (1999, p. 3) have felt it necessary to state that the drugs crisis is ongoing and unabated. Thus, a huge series of tasks continue to preoccupy the community and statutory sectors.

Just one of the many aspects associated with drugs has been crime. Quite separate to the problem of the illegality of drugs and the black market in which they are embedded, crime to raise money to buy drugs is a significant threat in the local communities of the north inner city. Just under 20 per cent of all cases receiving custodial sentences in Dublin district courts are for drugs-related offences (Bacik et al., 1998, p. 22). But Paul O'Mahoney (1993) argues that his research makes it abundantly clear that the large majority of drug users are imprisoned for theft and robbery and other forms of crime committed to raise money for drugs purchase. His argument has since been borne out by research undertaken by the Garda Research Unit which recorded that a majority of all people arrested, charged or suspected of criminal activity were drug users (Keogh, 1997). O'Mahoney found that, between 1986 and 1996, the percentage of prisoners in Mountjoy who were using drugs other than cannabis had risen from 37 per cent to 77 per cent, with opiate users in the majority (O'Mahoney, 1998, p. 60). Certainly, the majority of women in Mountjoy Prison are there for theft and drug-related offences and 71 per cent of them

come from inner city Dublin, with 42 per cent from the north inner city (Carmody and McEvoy, 1996).

Thus, while illegal drug use has driven many young people into
crime, it has done so at the expense of the families and communities where they live.

THE CONSTRUCTION OF MARGINALISED COMMUNITIES

Contemporary Irish society is commonly described as one which
has undergone a very rapid period of modernisation economically
and socially since the 1970s, changing from a largely agricultural
base to a largely service industry base. This progression, however,
has had a markedly different impact on people with lower skills
and educational levels, and has led to high levels of unemployment for them.

In Dublin as a whole, unemployment was four times greater in
1994 than in 1974, compared with only a doubling of that figure
nationally (Drudy and McLaren, 1996). For the micro-
communities of the north inner city, the situation was bleaker still.
The shift towards containerisation and, with it, the diminished
importance of the Dublin docks area by the beginning of the
1970s, were the first indications that jobs would vanish permanently. D. Connolly (1997, p. 24) points out that the range of work
listed in the 1971 Census for the inner city included:

- 27.3 per cent — producers, repairers and makers

- 23.6 per cent — labourers and unskilled workers

- 20.2 per cent — transport, communications and storage workers.

Bannon et al. (1981), in their landmark study of Dublin's urbanisation, noted that over 10,000 jobs were lost from the entire inner
city during the 1970s, as small local manufacturing faced widespread shutdown and the introduction of new technologies made
much of the unskilled and semi-skilled labour listed above redun-
dant. Unemployment rates for the inner city rose from 9.3 per
cent in 1971 to 12.1 per cent in 1979 to 31.8 per cent in 1991. This
represented 11,500 unemployed people in 1991, which by 1994 had
escalated to 14,530 people (D. Connolly, 1997, p. 25). In the micro-
communities, in 1987, unemployment rates in the ten north inner

city wards ranged from 17.2 per cent in Ballybough B to 56.2 per-cent in North Dock C (Alliance for Work Forum, n.d., p. 26). Over 85 per cent of the unemployed men had been so for more than one year (ibid., p. 27). A survey by the North Wall Community Associa-tion in 1981, 1984 and 1987 recorded levels of unemployment of 48.4 per cent, 58.2 per cent and 80 per cent respectively (ibid. , p. 35). The Youth Employment Action Group in Our Lady of Lourdes parish in Sean MacDermott Street carried out a survey in the par-ish in 1981 and established a 70 per cent rate of unemployment (YEAG press release, 11 April 1983).

From the early 1970s, rehousing of a substantial proportion of the population from unrehabilitated tenement dwellings managed by Dublin Corporation to the newly built local authority estates to the northwest, west and southwest of Dublin city led to a decline in population in the north inner city. The population that re-mained carried a much higher than average proportion of elderly people, many living alone. People had to learn to live with an in-creasing deterioration of the housing stock. In general, people lived in a higher-than-average percentage of multiple dwelling units of households with only two rooms, with a greater density of persons per room, compared with the greater Dublin area, and in housing that was overall in urgent need of renewal. Between 1966 and 1993, land use patterns in the north and south inner cities combined saw a decline in industrial space from 20 per cent to 6.5 per cent, a decline in wholesale space from 10 per cent to 5.3 per cent, and an increase in derelict space from 2 per cent to 13 per cent (D. Connolly, 1997, p. 18). The market-driven pressure to convert land use resulted in a decline of residential space from 35 per cent in 1966 to 25.6 per cent in 1993, with an upsweep of office use from 10 per cent to just under 20 per cent (ibid.).

The tradition of early school-leaving, which resulted from the accessibility of entry-level work in the labour market, continued on an uninterrupted trajectory, with tragic results for young peo-ple, who almost certainly faced a future of unemployment, along with older men whose jobs had been shed and who would never regain an economic foothold. A 1979 survey indicated that just over 64 per cent of the population had left school by the age of 15 and of those unemployed, 68 per cent had finished school by the age of 15 (ibid., p. 23). In that same year, there were only 37 pupils from Our Lady of Lourdes parish attending secondary school (Murphy-Lawless, 1983, p. 11). By 1991, just under 47 per cent of the working age population had left school by the age of 15; in four wards, over 66 per cent of the population had left school before the age of 16 (ibid.). As early as 1981, the Garda were recording that one-sixth of all crimes committed in the Republic were carried out in Area C of the north inner city (ibid.).

In a time of crisis, citizens and communities in a democratic society naturally turn to the institutions of their state, including the central and local administration as well as the legislature and the judiciary. But there was no substantive response from either national or local government to this deepening urban crisis of growing unemployment and the increasing dereliction and lack of re-investment in the inner city. The community itself did organise and respond as best it could. By 1975, 12 local tenants' associations began to protest against rising unemployment, the huge difficulties with housing and housing maintenance, and the proposed reallocation of land use for car parks and office blocks (Kelleher and Whelan, 1992, quoted in Curtin and Varley, 1997, pp. 397–8). This group, which became known as the North Centre City Community Action Project, objected strenuously to the development plans of Dublin Corporation and sought alternative expert views on how to re-build the north inner city in such a way as to strengthen the social fabric and community base which was under severe attack.

The independent TD elected from the local area, Tony Gregory, who worked with NCCCAP, brokered a deal with Charles Haughey in 1982, offering his support to vote in Haughey's minority Fianna Fáil government in exchange for the "Gregory Deal", which resulted in 440 new local authority houses being built in the area. This movement has been described as "citizen mobilisation", giving some "autonomy from the state" (ibid., p. 398). However, although the strength of this community development movement established a context for ongoing activist work in the area, the profile of multiple levels of deprivation has not substantially changed over a 20-year period and the state's engagement has been, in effect, far too little, far too late.

Since 1993 and the advent of the Celtic Tiger, and despite what has been a considerable drop in unemployment, economists estimate that "there remains a substantial legacy of long-term unemployment even in the face of record economic growth" (Fitzgerald and Ingoldsby, 1999, p. 5). The rise in numbers of jobs available in the inner city area has not significantly reduced unemployment for long-term residents there, because many of these new jobs were part of the expansion of skilled employment in sectors like the international financial services sector on the site of the old Dublin Docklands (ibid, p. 6). The Gamma area-based statistics to measure deprivation, using the 1996 Census for the entire inner city area covered by the Dublin Inner City Partnership, indicate that 43 per cent of the population left school before the age of 15, compared with 35 per cent in the state as a whole. Thirty-six per cent of the population in this area had either no formal education at all or primary education only, compared with 30 per cent for the state. The unemployment rate was 27.3 per cent in the area compared with 14.8 per cent in the state. Thirty-nine per cent of the total unemployed population had primary education only, compared with 33 per cent for the state. Twenty per cent of workers were classified as semi-skilled, compared with the national average of just over 13 per cent, while 19 per cent of the workforce were unskilled, over twice the national average. There was an increase of 23 per cent unemployment in the inner city between 1986 and 1996. The highest rate of unemployment at area level was in Mountjoy A at 59 per cent. This area also had more than twice the national average of youth unemployment, standing at 42 per cent. In the Gamma summary indicators of relative deprivation,[3] on a range from one to ten, the inner city as a whole ranked 7.0 in 1996, compared with 8.6 in 1991. However, in 1996, there were 17 wards still classified with a score of 9.0 or 10.0 (Gamma, Report No. 27, 1998).

From the 1970s, this nightmare scenario, the gutting of a local economy, its workers and its social relations, was repeated in more or less the same pattern in cities throughout Britain and the United States. André Gorz (1994) argues that this movement echoes previous waves of joblessness and de-skilling, such as that

---

[3] The list of indicators for the multiple deprivation index include: social class composition; education levels; unemployment levels, including long-term; proportion of lone parent families; and age dependency rates (Gamma, 1998).

which occurred in the late-nineteenth century. But this time, there appears to be a seismic shift. The complexity of current capitalism means that communities, cities and governments face markets which are more autonomous than ever before. Thus, it is less feasible than ever for communities and states to exercise any social control over what Gorz terms "the logic of the market", except of course as consumers.

So, at the same time, the way the work is now organised in the market means a downgrading of structures which once helped to sustain a sense of personal identity. As Gorz frames it, "Socialisation no longer guarantees individuals a place in a social order" (1994, p. 23). The core problem is that "increasingly efficient technologies [are] creating more and more wealth with less and less labour" (ibid., p. ix), bringing into question how we see ourselves as workers.

A number of social theorists have been preoccupied with this aspect of the current marketplace, including the sociologist Zygmunt Bauman. Bauman's deep concern is that, compared with the industrial phase of modernity, "the roads to self-identity, to a place in society, to life lived in a form recognisable as that of meaningful living" no longer include work but "daily visits to the market place" as a consumer. And, if you are one of the "new poor" for whom there will not be work, you can participate in the market in the most limited way possible because you have no money with which to become a major consumer (Bauman, 1998, p. 26). This is what social exclusion has come to mean.

For the philosopher Alphonso Lingis (1997), the only appropriate response to looking at what "the exclusion from skilled labour and high-tech industries" does to individuals and their communities is "anger and distress". But this anger and distress can also help to generate a community of protest.

HEROIN ENTERS IN

Heroin arrived into the north inner city in significant quantities sometime in the spring of 1981. It was thought subsequently that the social changes accompanying the Iranian Revolution opened the way to a hugely increased amount of heroin coming on the world market from Pakistan, Afghanistan, Burma and Laos, through new routes of distribution which were better secured and financed, thus creating a lucrative and ever expanding market.[4] In June 1982, the Minister for Health requested the then Medico-Social Research Board to carry out research on the reported increase in addicts in the north inner city of Dublin and the south inner city. There had been sporadic official concern about illegal drug usage in the 1960s and 1970s, with accompanying changes in the legislation governing controlled substances (Butler, 1991). But widespread opiate use was something of which there was no experience. The preliminary scoping work of the Medico-Social Research Board, tracking numbers and constructing a profile of heroin users in the north inner city emerged with the following picture: 9 per cent of the young population between the ages of 15 to 24 were using heroin, and the MSRB estimated from their street work that £100 or more was needed each day to maintain a seriously addicted individual. This scoping exercise was extended and 85 users were found from Mountjoy A Ward; the resulting data revealed a young population, almost all early school leavers, and virtually all unemployed (Dean et al., 1983). Reviewing the data now, one of its most interesting and overlooked aspects was that 68 of these 85 respondents reported that their first experience of heroin came through a friend or a relative. In other words, heroin use has occurred in an overwhelmingly familiar social context. This has not been the shadowy world of the unknown stranger pushing drugs so often portrayed in the media. These young people knew one another as schoolmates, as neighbours, as relatives.

However, the immediate concerns and responses of the state did not centre on the social setting of heroin use and its complexity. Despite an Eastern Health Board report in 1982 which asked questions about the poverty of the working-class areas where drug use had become such a marked feature and a 1983 Inter-Ministerial Task Force which also flagged these issues, there was no social prevention policy which concentrated on this dimension until the 1996 Ministerial Task Force.

Instead, the official policies which were implemented during the 1980s were largely to do with treatment and treatment facilities, in

---

[4] For an account of these changes, read A. McCoy (1991), *The Politics of Heroin.*

addition to thinking about the problem of supply reduction and policing. Treatment programmes were derived in the main from a
model which conceptualised drug use as an individual problem of
addiction. A shift in policy around 1991, to set up locally based
treatment centres, began to emphasise a harm reduction approach
to heroin. There was also a move to encourage increased co-
operation between interested voluntary and statutory bodies, with a
proportion of this work concentrated on the problems of supply reduction and demand reduction.

Critics of this approach argued that although locally based
treatment was very important, the community itself needed to
have real participation in the decision-making about service needs
in the area (McCann, 1998). In fact, the location of services without full community participation did on occasion lead to some
hostility about the fact that specific communities were labelled,
while at the same time the issues of social deprivation went unad-
dressed (Loughran, 1999, p. 313). As critics saw it, this "sidestep-
ping" (ibid.) of the social issues that lay behind extensive drug use
would be challenged in 1996.

In the meantime, in the north inner city there were many targeted efforts from the community and voluntary sector to try to
deal with the meanings of a developing heroin culture in the midst
of the ongoing economic disintegration of the area. In the early
1980s, Our Lady of Lourdes parish in Sean MacDermott Street
supported interventions like the Youth Employment Action
Group, which challenged the Industrial Development Authority's
Inner City Unit to develop replacement industries and to set up a
cluster factory at the end of Sean MacDermott Street. The action
group hoped that such small-scale industries could provide employment potential and real training for young people from the
area. The group argued that this type of intervention was crucial to
stemming the growing sub-culture of drug-related crime. Similarly, the Lourdes Youth and Community Services sought to develop locally based, locally managed and locally staffed youth and
community development schemes from the mid-1980s. Potentially
cohesive efforts like these continued to be frustrated, however, by
the lack of sufficient state response; without extensive state resources, especially in the area of training and development work,
too little could be set in motion.

In 1993, reflecting on the lack of response, ICON stated that if the "major economic and social issues" that lay behind the problem of heroin and drug use were not addressed, then the state would end up by doing what other countries had already done, namely building "a ring of steel around areas" to contain their worst effects (quoted in Loughran, 1999, p. 309).

This "ring-fencing" has been characterised by the French anthropologist Loïc Wacquant as the "accumulation of multiple deprivations within the same households and neighbourhoods, the shrinking of social networks and slackening of social ties", while the state withdraws to the most minimal provision of public assistance and social insurance, at the same time policing the most visible outcome of urban inequalities in the form of crime, with a growing prison population (Wacquant, 1993, p. 366). He cites the northeast Paris suburbs where the police and official state bureaucracy tend to dismiss local residents' needs as irrelevant, on the basis of their postal address alone. This unofficial policy has special meaning for young teenagers harassed by police who treat them as second-class citizens. Thus it is not alone the lack of money and possessions which characterise their poverty. For Wacquant, their poverty is also a form of social poverty where they are deprived of respect and equal treatment; where they instead experience themselves as social outcasts as they are deprived of the capacity to define their own identities (ibid., p. 368). The cumulative impacts of this "territorial stigmatisation" (ibid., p. 369) differ between European countries and the United States with the latter society, in Wacquant's judgement, further along the road to the withdrawal of any positive interest in or commitment by the state to intervene and to resolve structural inequalities.

Work by Phillipe Bourgois (1997) on crack cocaine in the poverty-stricken New York district of East Harlem documents the resulting damage of almost total state neglect. In his deeply pessimistic conclusion to his account of where he lived and worked for several years amongst a growing drugs culture, Bourgois argues that drug abuse is both "symptom" and "symbol" of the entrenched and complex dynamics of marginalisation and alienation. With an intensifying contrast between the minimum-wage unskilled service industry jobs which comprise the only available legitimate work to young people from the *barrio* in New York City and the money and relative autonomy that appear to be on offer from the extensive illegal drugs economy, he states that there must be a political will to re-motivate and redirect what is otherwise "crushed human potential" — crushed by poverty and powerlessness in mainstream society (ibid., p. 322).

Mercifully, Dublin's north inner city has not experienced the kind of complete public sector breakdown described by Bourgois. Throughout these decades, there has remained the potential to engage with the state, in spite of the increasing pressures at all levels.[5] The task to which it is hoped this report can contribute is to describe one of the "nested" contexts (Byrne, 1998)[6] in which the illegal drugs culture has flourished, in order to help inform understandings of where state actions now need to be directed to deal with both symbol and symptom.

In respect of drug use, the research project which is the sister piece to this current work looked in depth at heroin users in the north inner city and their accounts of how they had first come to engage with the drug (Coveney et al., 1999). This is an uneven process, highly dependent on what drugs were available on street markets at what time and on highly local conditions of social context and sets of friends. But what emerges as a constant in people's stories was that illegal drugs were *attractive*:

---

[5] Just one pressure relates to vastly increased workloads for public health nurses and social work teams that co-exists with a huge problem of understaffing.

[6] This term "nested" is one that the sociologist David Byrne (1998) uses to help describe the way the many components and variables of a social system are linked. For example, the statistics on educational attainment in the north inner city are poor compared with other areas of the country. This reflects interactions between the Department of Education and curriculum development committees and the school, between teachers and children in the school, and between school and home, all of which may make it more likely that the dominant peer group culture rejects the value of doing homework and of being a good student. Byrne points to the research which has tracked this movement, where the mean hours of homework done by the *entire* school population matter more for the achievement of individual students than the actual hours of homework done by the *individual* student (Byrne, 1998, p. 133–134). His point is that in order to change that dominant culture, we need to understand all the interactions, and to ensure that the educational resource pool is redefined as widely as possible to include everyone's inputs, immaterial and material, in all these "nested" contexts. This is not simply a linear process of achievement or non-achievement in school in an evenly distributed pattern each year.

Interview data indicated that the involvement of young people in heroin appeared to be fuelled by a volatile combination of a ready availability of the drug and a changing and expansive sub-culture which rates being "stoned" or "wrecked" high in importance. Young people were building a social life around heroin use in the context of a bleak socio-economic outlook for inner city communities. Many were deliberately seeking an alternative lifestyle (ibid., 1999, p. 5).

In other words, the nested contexts of heroin use were not just what may appear to be the obvious negative ones of poverty, powerlessness and unemployment. Getting engaged in illegal drug use appeared to be a *positive* activity, one which delivered pleasure and satisfied curiosity. As a result, the lethal impact of addiction was a long way removed from young people's thoughts when they first used.

But use patterns have also changed considerably since the early 1980s. The most significant change has been the growth of the dance and club culture since the late 1980s underpinned by the use of ecstasy ("E"). For a minority of "E" users, this has involved smoking heroin to come down from a night's dancing and using "E". There was a steady growth upwards in the number of young people seeking treatment for addiction through smoking heroin (O'Brien and Moran, 1997, p. 41), which phenomenon puzzled researchers (ibid.). At the time, there was no extant published research profile of ecstasy users and the sub-group who smoked heroin in tandem with their "E" use. That research has since begun to come on stream and indicates the fleet-footedness of both the young people's drug sub-culture and the drugs market itself (Coveney et al., 1999; McElrath and McEvoy, 1999; Mayock, 2000; Murphy-Lawless et al., 2000). The line spoken by the schoolgirl character, Diane, to the former heroin user, Mark, in the film *Trainspotting* — "the world's changing, music's changing, even drugs are changing" — captures that aspect of illegal drug use which proves so attractive to young people, precisely because it is exciting, part of a search for a "high" or a "buzz" and where young people are always seeking new horizons. The music club called The Asylum, which was located in Sackville Place off O'Connell Street, brought together the music, the drugs and this excitement for many young people in the inner city in the early 1990s. In the summer of 1994, I interviewed a young man who worked in the club as a bouncer and his detailed descriptions of the line-up of drug dealers as one entered the club, and the room above the dance space reserved for smokers wanting a place to come down after a night's dancing to hardcore "techno" music, were later re-counted to me by a number of respondents in two subsequent projects (see Coveney et al., 1999 and Murphy-Lawless et al., 2000). Bouncers like this man were witness to the turf wars between larger dealers, not infrequently accompanied by threats and violence that could break out at the club. But this much more dubious aspect of illegal drug consumption did not necessarily impinge on or change the decision-making of young people who were otherwise anxious to experiment with whatever was on offer.

The sister study (Coveney et al., 1999) makes it clear that many young people are prepared to experiment widely with illegal drug use, that they are prepared to take their chances over the issue of the quality of the street drugs they buy and that they are prepared to mix drug cocktails almost indiscriminately. In many ways, the explosion of dance music enabled heroin to be woven into a new pattern of consumption and new generations of users, far removed in image terms from the addict injecting himself or "shooting up", as it is known, in a derelict house or street corner. Hence with the rise in numbers of those seeking treatment as heroin smokers, there was a reported drop in the age of those users as styles changed (O'Brien and Moran, 1997).

In this series of situations and settings where the state was always going to lag behind these rapidly evolving youth styles, the state's engagement here again was far too little, far too late. It was not the Department of Health and Children, for example, but ICON, through its Inter-Agency Drugs Project, which pressed for special programme treatment facilities to be set up for smokers (ICON, 1999). The most recent estimates of opiate drug use in the greater Dublin area was 13,460 people (CityWide, 1999, p. 3). Since 1996, the state has finally come to acknowledge that to respond to widespread illegal drug use means that it must also respond to the social and economic contexts where that drug use is located. But it is the communities which have challenged the state to take on that vital perspective.

THE IMPACT ON WOMEN OF LIVING WITH HEROIN: FOCUS OF THIS STUDY

Since 1997, a number of research studies have begun to redress what was a dearth of published information on women and gendered patterns of drug use, so that it is now clear that in inner city Dublin, heroin use is far from being an overwhelmingly male undertaking. The recognition of the need for family support services for women drug users, coming first from the Ana Liffey Project, has expanded the meaning of treatment to include such pressing realities of women's lives as the need to incorporate crèche facilities in treatment centres (Moran, 1999). As early as 1994, it was argued that family and community support, even in areas ravaged by the crisis, was still significant and that women living as single parent units did have access to an extended family structure (Ana Liffey Drug Project, 1994, pp. 12–13; ICON, 1994, p. 72). However, the nature and degree of support for women was not researched and individuals and communities alike reported fear and apathy about living with the drugs crisis (ICON, 1994, p. 38). It was evident that such strong reactions were unlikely to exist in isolation from how women live their daily lives and carry out their family work.

The ethnography presented here set out to explore what those patterns are with women. In contrast with its sister study, here the focus of enquiry has not been heroin use itself but how ordinary everyday life, specifically ordinary life for women, has been influenced by the growth of the illegal heroin culture and economy in the north inner city, amidst all the other ravages of economic marginalisation recounted above.

Coveney and Sheridan (1996) have convincingly argued that women in the inner city continue to face an uphill struggle in establishing an independent context for themselves in both the family setting and the workplace setting. In the former, women continue to bear the major portion of unpaid and unacknowledged household and family-building work, including the care of children; in the latter, their work is very low-paid and unskilled and they face severe barriers to breaking through into better workplace settings. These include the lack of education, the lack of flexibility in workplace arrangements and the negative attitudes of their male partners and husbands towards any disruption of traditional gender roles (ibid.).

The surmise that lay behind this current study was that living with heroin in the family and in the community creates even greater strain on the lives of women. Of course, living with long-term unemployment and then heroin as well has placed enormous strains on men and on their traditional roles. But the emphasis in this study is on women because women are still by and large the ones who carry out the main work of caring and nurturing. And, because women have been especially active in organising them-selves in local self-development groups, which have often led on to local community-based projects, a study of how they have coped both within the family and the community group may have impor-tant lessons about achieving comprehensive and long-term par-ticipation across all levels of the community (including the par-ticipation of men who have been traditionally hesitant about such involvement).

In the sister study on heroin users, people recounted how they had to try to come to terms with the impact that their personal heroin use had on their families. This suggested that women who must respond to heroin and other illegal drug use because of their family involvement or their concern to prevent younger members of their family being involved would have special needs. It was also thought likely that a family involvement with heroin might badly affect relationships and support within the extended family, and beyond that in the community, as women tried to negotiate the many pressures of responding to their partners, sons and daughters, and nieces and nephews.

In the context of drugs, women's multiple roles as family mem-bers can become very complex: they may have to confront the drug economy as mothers, sisters, carers, partners of users, users themselves. They can be dealing with the problems thrown up by a partner or older sibling attending a treatment programme while a child/younger sibling is experimenting with drug use. A woman drug user may face specific problems organising her drug-related needs around her commitments as a parent, especially when young children are involved. Organising the money to buy street drugs, whether as a user or a parent trying to help a user, can be hazardous and time-expensive. Yet another dimension to the drugs crisis for women has been the reality of prison sentences for themselves or their family members. Prison sentences for drug-related offences cut across familial networks and can make further demands on women as mothers and carers.

As indicated above, the illegal drug economy has generated huge levels of revenue which must also have entailed different expectations and outcomes. Younger teenagers were actively involved in street dealing in the early to mid-1990s, for example. There has remained a critical challenge of the creation of stable long-term employment possibilities in the north inner city to motivate young people, which must have been a huge weight of concern for women anxious to secure their children's futures free of involvement with heroin.

The object of this study was to construct an ethnographic account to explore these contexts as fully as possible, and also to explore how some women were thinking their way through these dilemmas at personal and community level, in order to emerge with a clearer understanding of where state policy must be challenged to develop better support structures for women, men, their families and the community in the immediate future.

Summary of Chapter One

♦ *The north inner city has had to live with the social and economic damage inflicted by widespread heroin use since the beginning of the 1980s. The introduction of heroin into a community already experiencing a process of change imposed by the decline of traditional industries in the area, forced a readjustment to almost every aspect of everyday life for individuals and families living there.*

♦ *Illegal heroin use and large-scale heroin dealing have had a major impact on the local economy and have represented a huge source of revenue. In 1993/4, it was estimated that the annual circulation of money directly connected to the heroin economy was £9.1 million in the north-east inner city alone.*

♦ *The number of users from the north inner city entering treatment has risen steadily. In the sister study to this current study, it was estimated in 1998 that there was a prevalence rate of 20.44 heroin users per 1,000 of the population in the north inner city and it was stated that this was a clear under-estimation of users, covering almost exclusively only those in treatment with registered agencies at that time. According to the national drugs reporting system, there were 687 opiate users registered for treatment in the North Inner City Elec-toral Borough in 1998.*

♦ *Two of the voluntary umbrella groups responding to the drugs crisis, ICON and the CityWide Drugs Crisis Campaign, stated in 1999 that this crisis is ongoing in its impact. ICON has stated special concern about the lack of necessary re-sources, short-term and long-term, to deal with the impact of heroin. Just one aspect of this is the rise in drugs-related crime, with recent statistics indicating that the majority of people detained by the Garda and the majority of those im-prisoned for theft and robbery are drug users.*

♦ *These young people are raising money for their drug habit in communities which have experienced the stark reality of se-vere economic marginalisation since the beginning of the 1970s. In that decade alone, over 10,000 jobs were lost in Dublin's inner city and record levels of long-term unemploy-ment were already being recorded by the beginning of the 1980s. This sharp economic decline went hand-in-hand with deteriorating housing stock and the disruption and relocation of many people from the north inner city communities to the new suburbs. Other signs of the deepening urban crisis, like the rise in numbers of disaffected early school leavers, drew an insufficient response from the state throughout that dec-ade while the numbers of heroin users increased. In 1996, 17 wards in the inner city as a whole were scaled, using sum-mary indicators of deprivation on a range of one to ten, with a score of nine or ten.*

♦ *Despite a considerable expansion in the labour force in the inner city since the early 1990s, this has not affected the status of the long-term unemployed. There was an increase of unemployment of 23 per cent between 1986 and 1996 in the inner city and the highest rate of unemployment in 1996 was registered in Mountjoy A Ward at 59 per cent.*

♦ *This level of urban crisis, with industry bases shifting to high-technology, highly-skilled labour, has led to what appears to be the near-permanent exclusion of people who grew up in the traditional industrial base and to the stripping away of a stable identity between a person, the work they do, and the community where they live. Many social theorists are concerned about the profound effects this has on the lives of individuals and families and how this fracturing of communities impacts on social integration.*

♦ *At its most stark, the problem has been defined in this way: what is now important to a growth economy is that people are consumers and that consumption boosts the economy. But if you are one of the "new poor" without work or with very limited access to work because you have come from those traditional forms of work which no longer exist, then you are socially excluded because you cannot consume on the same scale.*

♦ *The connections between the declining social and economic base of the north inner city and the growth in the heroin culture were not part of the official government response to the drugs problem for more than 15 years. Resources, when they began to be invested, were concentrated instead on the treatment of the individual's problem of addiction. For the most part, it was local voluntary agencies and groups which tried to develop a series of responses to the special problems that fuelled the growth of a heroin sub-culture. The concern of these groups was that if the difficult social and economic issues that marred the north inner city were not dealt with, the wider community, represented by the state, would simply try to build a "ring of steel" around the area to contain its worst effects.*

♦ *This "ring-fencing" of localities where jobs have gone, social networks have been destroyed and illegal drugs have entered in are characteristics of many cities in Europe and the United States. The outcome of deep social inequalities in the urban areas has led to entrenched patterns of alienation and, at its worst, to a growing prison population. Above all, what has* been lacking in cities like New York, where the state operates the bare minimum of services in the poorest areas, has been the political will and extensive state action to help a re-building process.

♦ In many ways, the depth of alienation described elsewhere as the result of a stripping-down of basic state services of health, education and assistance, has not taken place to the same extent in Dublin's north inner city. And yet, drugs remain highly attractive to young people in the inner city; because drugs fashions and use patterns change, new forms of drug use have become popular indicated, for example, by an increase in the number of people who smoke heroin, often as an addition to their use of ecstasy. So young people are building an alternative identity for themselves amidst a local economy which offers them little by way of legitimate, skilled work for their futures.

♦ The state, through its central and local government departments and state-sponsored bodies, has been slow to respond to or even to understand these changes, and it was a community group, ICON, which urged that special treatment programmes be set up for smokers in 1996. Only since 1996 has the full social and economic context of illegal drug use begun to be acknowledged by the state.

♦ This very complicated environment of no secure work for families over three decades, the widespread drugs culture and the increasing marginalisation of a community has had a huge impact on family and community structures. The ethnography which is presented here set out to explore the way these complex events impinged on women as mothers and carers, in particular the way heroin has affected them and their family lives. The object of the study was to explore how women were responding to these dilemmas at personal level, with their families and in their communities. It is hoped that the study findings will contribute to a clearer understanding of where the state must be challenged to develop better support structures for women, men, their families and their community.

Chapter Two

RESEARCHING THE EVERYDAY OF WOMEN'S LIVES

THE CREATION OF SOCIOLOGICAL KNOWLEDGE

The sociologist Zygmunt Bauman writes that we live our everyday lives "deeply immersed in our daily routines . . . we hardly ever pause to think about the meaning of what we have gone through, even less often have we the opportunity to compare our private experience with the fate of others, to see the social in the individual, the general in the particular" (1990, p. 10).

This study is about women who have thought about their everyday lives as mothers and about that central role in family life. As Chapter One makes clear, these roles have been lived out in the midst of a deep social crisis in the north inner city, a painful restructuring of a community which has been largely frozen out of a changing labour market for three decades; these same three decades have seen the rise and rise of illegal heroin use and the illegal market that accompanies it. This drastic restructuring has taken place without the say or inputs of people living there.

Women living in the north inner city have been forced to pause and think about how they are living because of the problematic, often profoundly painful, experiences this dynamic has created for them. Many women have worked hard to make sense of their individual life stories and needs; to connect these up to an analysis of the collective needs of their community. In an immediate and real way, the women encountered in the course of this study are experts about many aspects of what their family and the community needs as the latter attempts to take back comprehensive control of its own space and to support women and men in the work of sustaining family life.

When women meet to reflect on what they have been doing, whether it is community work or group support work or training that brings them together, they are actually doing the bones of sociology and social research. Sociology is the study of what has and is happening; it is the attempt to understand and make sense, in a methodical way, community and the lives of individuals. Its goal and the goal of this report are to see, with the help of the cumulative knowledge that has been gained, where we can go from here in seeking change.

Everyday lives often hold the most important information in identifying what needs to change. Taking one step back from daily life, "defamiliarising the familiar", often enables people to identify carefully the coping strategies which they have been forced to adopt to protect family life. These have become so much a part of each day that they almost become invisible. Bauman (1990, p. 13) argues that when people begin to pull together many stories, this process is a good analytical tool for making links between each story, for recognising the commonly used strategies, "the levels of our daily concerns", and thus recognising how we "struggle for more control over our plight". This is sociological knowledge.

By laying out the complexity of the stories, this knowledge can also help to identify points where the larger social system, which contains these daily rhythms, can be challenged to support a process of positive change.

Here, the work of another sociologist, David Byrne, can be helpful. Byrne, who has had the life-long experience of living and working in Newcastle, a depressed industrial town in north-east England that has fallen on ever harder times, says that we need a non-linear model to describe the complexity of change in a given social locality. He sees the individual household as "the significant social unit in which we spend our lives" (Byrne, 1998, p. 101). At the same time, the changes and movements of each household take place in a social space which is complex in a way that cannot be explained by simple cause-and-effect linear models. Hence, there is the need for a descriptive non-linear model to explain change in individual households and the community. There are interactive or contingent effects which connect up, rely on and create emerging circumstances which are unpredictable.

A non-linear model would try to include or name most or all of the elements which have contributed, for example, to the recent history of the north inner city in Dublin. Drawing on the discussion in Chapter One, a list of these would include (at the very least) the following aspects:

- A permanent shift away from skilled and semi-skilled manual work, resulting in a massive increase in male unemployment (examples of which would be the introduction of containerisation in the docks; the downgrading of Coras Iompair Eireann (CIE) as a contractor for moving goods; the removal of the An Post Sorting Office from Sheriff Street);

- Urbanisation and development plans from the mid-1970s onwards which ignored the importance of local community;

- Poor, non-renewable housing stock, with the exception of new housing schemes secured under the Gregory Deal in the early 1980s;

- Failure of the schooling system to adequately take on the needs of inner-city working-class children, as secondary education became widely available;

- Tradition of early school-leaving in the inner city;

- Introduction of wide-scale marketing of heroin from 1980 onward with expanded markets stemming from huge increases in poppy cultivation in Pakistan, Afghanistan, Burma and Laos;

- Failure of the state to respond systematically and comprehensively to community demands, including the demand for youth employment schemes during the first wave of the heroin epidemic in 1982–4;

- Feminisation of the labour market; remaining jobs open to families from the inner city from the 1980s onwards were low-skilled women's work, like contract cleaning;

- Gentrification of the inner city initiated by the Docklands Development and building of apartment complexes from the end of the 1980s.

This list could be extended greatly. However, the point of it is that all of these are multi-dimensional relationships with complex interactive effects over time, so that at the level of each household, families have been impacted and involved in different ways.

Thus, for example, this study has concentrated on women whose families have been affected by all these factors. But some have experienced direct impact where children took up heroin use; some indirect impact, where playspace for children was restricted by formal closure of what few facilities there were and where there was a need to protect young children from heroin users in the immediate street-spaces near their houses and flats.

At the same time these events were reshaping the north inner city, there was an inability and, often, an outright refusal of bodies from outside the locality to respond comprehensively to this complexity. Local actors could see much of the complexity, but because they lacked sufficient political resources to challenge substantively this lack of response, they had to struggle even harder to build the basis for a more collective approach.[1]

The spread of the heroin sub-culture has been a crisis for a community already suffering from a high level of inequality. However, points of crisis have the potential for "decisive change" (Bauman, 1999, p. 141); because a crisis means that "things cannot stay as they are", Byrne argues that what appear to be "small disturbances or developments" can bring about transformation, one in which people can exercise agency over the way matters unfold from crisis (1998, p. 41–2).

Things have not stayed the same for the north inner city, but if there is to be an operable and decent future for the families there, much more must change. This study documents a major source of agency and change in that community: women themselves.

STUDY METHODOLOGY: THE ETHICS OF WOMEN INTERVIEWING WOMEN

The methodology for this study was an ethnographic one, where having made contact with appropriate groups and individuals, and

---

[1] Here the work of the NCCCAP, ICON, and the Inter-Agency Drugs Project, amongst other local projects, was crucial prior to the summer of 1996.

obtained their agreement about participation in the study, the research team was in a position to maintain contact over a prolonged period of time in the locality, make fieldwork notes after each encounter and to work towards a situation of trust where in-depth individual and group interviews could be undertaken and recorded on audio-tape.

This approach requires a clear ethical sense, not least because women can confide quite easily in other women, including researchers, and are thus open to exploitation (Finch, 1984). The problem of exploitation came up almost at once in the course of this research. I encountered a number of women who had opened their hearts and experiences to a writer from outside the area who had preserved neither confidentiality nor respect. There were other problems of confidentiality for women at local level, where initial efforts to deal with the drugs problem had led on occasion to a breakdown of rules about personal and private disclosures, exposing individuals to dangerous levels of ridicule and isolation. As one interviewee put it, "The minute you walk up to that _____, everyone knows your business".

So there was an understandable reluctance and sense of caution about the research on the part of many people, even though the research team was approaching possible participants through local networks, where a person's credentials and previous work could be readily scrutinised.

Some potential participants expressed anxiety about the direction the work might take. We were cautioned that the research could easily be used against women by those who might want to judge that women had failed their families and we were asked to ensure that this did not happen. One of the questions put to the team at a very early point was what value the research could really have for such women; for unless a final report could be fed into developing strategies, it would be a waste of people's time.

This range of ethical issues, and also the issue of how the researcher controls the writing-up, ran like a thread throughout the fieldwork period. Every participant was given an undertaking that the draft report would be submitted to them, to see if there was material they wanted to have taken out and not used. Yet, in my very last interview, a group session, the problem of confidentiality was still troubling women, as if it had been a first meeting with me.

Throughout the fieldwork period, some women felt little confidence in the research, possibly because the nature of their coming together involved the core of the trauma that heroin brings to women's lives, namely, the loss of their children to the drug, to the way of life that accompanies it, and the consequent impact on family life. For others, the focus of their community work perhaps made the research process easier. Involvement in community work to improve local conditions appeared to enable women to take a step back from what were often extremely painful personal issues.

A number of women responded to the interviews and meetings with great energy. And everyone who participated in the research was convinced of two important aspects:

- That it was important for people in official positions of authority to listen very carefully to their experiences because as one woman stated it, "Women are the backbones of the community";

- That it was important to put the problems in front of those in positions of authority who do not live with heroin on an ongoing basis, and thus who do not understand its impact.

One woman said at the outset:

> *The government has abandoned it [heroin] big time as a problem. I don't know what can be done about it. I don't know whether your report can make a difference. I hope it does. I hope they recognise that there are people like us out there.*

Yet there were a number of limitations on the data. The energetic critiques were generally directed outwards, rather than towards critical and contradictory aspects of family life. There were many issues that women did not bring up at all in the course of the fieldwork, like abusive physical and sexual relationships. It was clear that the work of mothering continued to provide a strong framework of explanation for their daily life, and that husbands and adult children who were emotionally dependent on them often proved to be a burden. At the same time, the work of tending them gave a *raison d'être* to women. Although perceived roles for women are changing amongst a younger generation of females in Ireland, the vast majority of women still go on to give birth, and as Pat O'Connor (1998, p. 137) argues, many of those women continue to find or create an identity for themselves in family and in caring work. The women in this study located themselves in that tradition.[2]

A major problem was that the women who engaged in the research represented only a small proportion of women in the community. The experiences of women who are coping on their own, women who have not become part of a group or community project for all sorts of reasons, are not necessarily reflected in the voices of those women who did participate. This is certainly true of one special group of women, those who are mothers and drug users. As Diane Hogan has argued, they face extremely stressful circumstances in carrying out their parenting, even compared with non-using mothers from the same socioeconomic background. A lack of confidence in caring for their children appears to be especially marked (Hogan and Higgins, 2001).

The research team had to deal with other problematic aspects of an ethnographic approach. Being in people's homes was felt to be too intrusive, except where an invitation was given freely by the participant. We could not presume to drop in anywhere without prior permission. We checked each time about the availability of meeting with women, no matter what the setting. Even so, our attendance at group meetings and events by appointment was invasive at times. A number of the women were involved in ongoing work with a variety of specific initiatives in the community and their meetings were held to facilitate that work, not to facilitate the research as such. So members of the research team might occupy a somewhat uncomfortable fly-on-the wall position on such occasions, hoping to be as unobtrusive as possible. Where group sessions were specifically called together for the purposes of the research, this still required that women give up their valuable time for several hours.

---

[2] Of course it is not possible to know, if a broader range of social and educational options had been available to the participants at an earlier point in their lives, whether they would have committed themselves completely to that caring role.

Aware of these difficulties, the research team maintained relationships throughout the fieldwork that were formal and respect-
ful rather than informal. The ethnography that resulted then was
strictly boundaried, in order to preserve that sense of respect.
These boundaries and constraints also made sense, given that the
research team was a group of outsiders, not from the local community. Yet the outsider status was balanced with some depth of
knowledge both about being a mother and about the locality. Two
of the team members had long connections with the north inner
city going back to the late 1960s, one with family connections.

I had worked in the north inner city on and off since my early
twenties, running an out-of-school tutorial programme for primary school children in the late 1960s. This was where I first became aware of the work of mothering as an intense activity and
the extent to which women actively helped one another in that
work. In the early 1980s, I was involved with training and evaluation as part of a young people's employment action group set up
specifically to try to create opportunities as a counterweight to a
growing heroin sub-culture. Again, I encountered women who
were doing their work as mothers against a growing set of odds.
Each time research work returned me to the north inner city in the
early and mid-1990s, I was aware that the odds had lengthened
yet again for many women. I saw this deepening turmoil as a
mother myself who is committed to doing that work well and the
initial intention in undertaking this study was to see how women
in very difficult circumstances could be supported better in that
work. I interviewed and listened to accounts of daily life that were
frequently interwoven with desperate loss, due to circumstances
which were beyond the control of any one woman.

Of course, there are huge ethical issues in then writing up such
a report, especially with a small qualitative sample (Ford and
Reutter, 1990). Much recent writing in feminist social research
has explored the dilemmas and contradictions, as Michelle Fine
writes, of "whose lives get displayed" and "whose lives get protected by social science" (Fine, 1994, p. 73). She argues that the
spotlight has too often been turned on those who have the problems, with a corresponding lack of attention to the dysfunctional
state authorities like welfare offices and so on which have created
the problems. The women participants in this study have expert

voices about the dysfunctional nature of the very agencies which should have provided help, but which in fact worsened their circumstances. Of course, this carries the potential of disintegrating into a culture of blame and even passivity. But the participants were in fact very active at many levels in their community and their critique draws on all those experiences. One objective of this report is to give that critique as wide a hearing as possible. From that perspective, the ethical concern of invading people's lives is set off against the challenge of turning the spotlight on these institutions and agencies through interviewing and life histories.

Feminists like Anne Williams (1990) write about the researcher being able to construct an understanding of a complex situation which can only arise from the willingness of women to be interviewed in an open-ended manner. But the researcher/writer must also have a willingness to use their language and their concepts in constructing the written understanding of their world. It is a very delicate balance between taking over people's stories, restructuring their voices as Fine (1994) puts it, and enabling their stories to be heard. It does leave the writer in a position of power which is why it is critical that women have the final say on what material does or does not get used in the report. And if qualitative research in forms like ethnography can contribute to bring about social change, as I believe it can, there is no choice about writing as respectfully and carefully as possible. As Kathleen Lynch (1999, p. 49) has argued about this:

> It is possible to create knowledge and understanding through partnership between the researcher and the research subject, while recognising the differences between the two positions. The fact that the subject is co-creator of the knowledge means that they can exercise control over definitions and interpretations of their lifeworld.

It should also be stated that the women who were interviewed as part of this project have many different roles to play in their daily lives. This is a study of women who are making a difference in their lives and the lives of others, by creating possibilities of support out of almost insupportable burdens. These are women who are "honest storytellers" (Fine, 1994, p. 71) of their circumstances, women who are building and re-building their capacities and identities as individuals and as groups.

The feminist anthropologist Carol Stack (1996) writes about "the work of kinship" where women as mothers, friends and neighbours become "kin" as they help one another to take responsibility for their children and their worries about their children. Stack found that these networks were critical for women living under acute economic and social pressures and trying to organise a welfare rights organisation at local level in the United States. Stack argues that telling the story of such networks can contribute to a "progressive and feminist agenda", even though many stories are condensed in the process of writing:

> As feminist ethnographers, we take on a knotty paradox of social responsibility. We are accountable for the consequences of our writing, fully cognisant that the story we construct is our own (Stack, 1996, p. 106).

For me, the ethical basis for this study is gathering support for women who continue to do the work of mothering, despite the structures which have damaged them and their families, and thereby helping them to confront more comprehensively the practices which continue to damage them, including the ill effects of heroin. In writing up the various chapters, I have tried to stay as close as possible to the themes and concepts expressed by the women who spoke to us. This is important. As Ruth Behar has written:

> When you write vulnerably, others respond vulnerably. A different set of problems and predicaments arise which would never surface in response to more detached writing (Behar, 1996, p. 16).

"MATERNAL THINKING": WOMEN AS MOTHERS

One of the few feminist writers in the 1980s to view motherhood as having positive potential was Sara Ruddick. Ruddick is especially interested in how "maternal thinking", as she calls it (1989; 1993), can be part of creating social change. Ruddick has argued that for many people, becoming a mother entails a commitment that reshapes one's mind and one's life. This commitment will differ at different times in a woman's life, she writes, dependent on the numbers of children, their ages, their involvements, and her other involvements, but nonetheless it tends to continue rather than cease.[3] Ruddick argues that a huge number of women take up mothering in extremely difficult circumstances, where they must rear their children in the teeth of poverty and bigotry and even tyranny in many countries. Yet no matter how different the social and cultural circumstances, she identifies common themes on a daily basis that women practice as mothers:

> Mothers think out strategies of protection, nurturance and training. Like any other profession, a mother engages in a discipline. She asks certain questions relevant to her aims . . . Maternal thinking like other disciplines establishes criteria for determining failure and success, sets priorities, and identifies virtues necessary to the discipline (Ruddick, 1993, p. 238).

For Ruddick, a woman as a mother is as much a professional thinker as an academic or a scientist. Ruddick sees women as active, thinking agents, testing what they have to do in a very practical way in their everyday lives. They reflect on their work, they make judgements and decisions about their work, just as any other professional does. She notes that of course they frequently fail in their objectives for their children, for reasons over which they have little or no control, often making their experiences as mothers far from positive.

In the context of this study, for example, when women experienced failure, what they could not control were the complex changes in the north inner city which left their children vulnerable and their parents unable to protect them, a truly disempowering experience. One participant said of this:

---

[3] Ruddick also argues that this work, with the obvious exception of the biological work of pregnancy and birth, could be gender-free work in which men could be equally involved. But practically speaking, most "mothers" in the world at present are women. The role of fathers in family life and in the community did come up for discussion in the course of fieldwork and will be referred to in Chapter Four.

You don't really ever expect anything to happen to your children, I mean you don't expect your children to do this, especially when you're after rearing them hard. And you gave them all the love and you gave them anything you could, maybe tried to give them what they needed. You could never give them what they wanted, all of what they wanted, but if you tried to give them some of the things they needed. But I mean when you do all that for them and you give them plenty of love and you give them your heart and soul, and then for this, to turn round for this to happen, and it's devastating. And I think a person would have to go through it to realise what it's like.

Here is as vivid a description of maternal thinking, reflecting and decision-making as Ruddick might hope to find. Here also is the stark reality of a mother who has been up against the situation of widespread heroin use in a community with minimal options for its young people.

One of the disturbing aspects of women's work as mothers over the last 100 years or more is the way it has been policed by various expert authorities; medical doctors, psychologists, social workers and other officials of the state have all had something to say about how well or how badly women mother. Jolly (1998, p. 8) writes that formal "inspections" of mothers by such bodies "have rarely been positive for women". The western state has been good at allocating blame and fostering maternal guilt. Working-class mothers have been especially "singled out for maternal deficiency" wherever there were large-scale social problems, and women have been condemned as if they were personally responsible for these problems, like that of inadequate housing (ibid.). For Jolly, the record clearly indicates that women were often labelled for the "simple fact" of having to be mothers and workers at the same time, carrying the dual burden of tending home and children as well as earning wages.

Patricia Kennedy (1997, 1998) has also heavily criticised the state for its often wilful refusal to recognise the many pressures that the several dimensions of women's lives as mothers inevitably entail. In her three-dimensional model of these roles, Kennedy cites women's overlapping work as carers, earners and lifegivers. Each of these roles carries many challenges. For women in less than ideal circumstances, the challenges are colossal. Yet, Kennedy argues, the state chooses to privatise and thus ignore many elements of mothers' work so that its social policies are severely limited and far removed from the realities of women's lives. In calling for a "new politics of motherhood" Melissa Benn concurs with this position. She writes:

> I do not think our society/culture possesses a genuine understanding — or more to the point, a care — for what it means to raise a child, the quality of that experience, the quantity of effort involved (Benn, 1998, p. 18).

The women interviewed revealed a multiplicity of tasks that characterises their lives which could extend the categories of Kennedy's model with many subdivisions of time and caring labour. Within the three basic roles of carer, earner, life-giver, women spoke of their work as:

- Mothers
- Wives
- Grandmothers
- Aunts
- Sisters
- Neighbours
- Workers
- Counsellors
- Community activists
- Anti-drugs activists
- Trainees
- Trainers.

This list indicates that women who talked with us do not see themselves as mothers solely concerned about or victimised by living with heroin, even at crisis points. One woman was pregnant at the time her daughter, who was using heroin, was also giving birth.

She had to deal with her own baby's stillbirth, at the same time dealing with the many complications of her daughter's life. We met women who have passed through multiple crises as a result of their children's heroin use, but who have learned to cope. We also met younger women with young children who have not been tested in that direct way and who were hoping through their community work to build something better for their children to avoid the crisis of heroin. They are proud, strong, competent women who have had to learn far more than they might ever have wanted to learn about the impact of illegal drugs on a community. And they have not given up.

WOMEN'S CARING WORK: ITS POTENTIAL FOR POLITICAL CHANGE

If we are to challenge the state to mount an effective and coherent social policy to positively support the work of mothering and parenting, Ellen Ross, the social historian is certain that we will have to first "tell the hard things about motherhood" (Ross, 1995, p. 399). We will also need to communicate to a wider audience meaningful data about "the mother as a subject, a person with her own needs, feelings and interests" (ibid.).

Alison Jaggar, for one, makes a direct connection between emotion and the potential to see the world differently, to want to see it be a different world. Jaggar is certain that the traditional dismissal of emotion, especially women's emotions, as unimportant and not appropriate in the public world is itself unacceptable. Strong feelings, emotion and anger, are not just reactions. They are active ways of seeing and evaluating what is wrong about a prevailing state of affairs, seeing that differently, and seeing the need for change (Jaggar, 1989). Such strong emotions are not "conventionally acceptable" and those who experience what she calls these "outlaw" emotions are frequently individuals in a subordinate or disadvantaged position who have already paid a high personal price, living in a situation that the wider society chooses not to have challenged or debated. But if these outlaw emotions are shared and validated with others who feel in a similar way, this can be the basis for political action which can subvert or overturn the very situations that the dominant class would prefer to ignore.

In the course of the fieldwork, we encountered a lot of "outlaw emotions" which women have used in this active sense, channelling them to a variety of collective actions to bring about change in their lives. This is what I was seeking to document in undertaking the study because, like other feminist social scientists, I believe these accounts can lead to greater understanding and can be a focus for demanding more sensitive support from the state.

Ross argues that although it is often difficult to convey the complexities of the world of mothering, "the stories of mothers can have enormous political impact when they do tell them in public arenas" (1995, p. 400). She quotes from Arnlaug Leira's study of the Scandinavian welfare state about how mothers act as a "buffer zone" between family needs and the state, doing most of the informal work and services which are part of the costs of reproduction but which the state rarely wishes to acknowledge, not least because of its reluctance to absorb those costs in its budgets.

David Morgan (1996, pp. 177–8) has also written about the way women in effect do work for the state, how women are often given "particular responsibility in mediating between the public and the private across the threshold of the home". It is women who frequently are the doers of what Morgan terms "family practices", the "little fragments of daily life which are part of the normal taken-for-granted existence" and which can be sources of identity and stability.

Daily work, as a form of caring for family members, can also be seen to constitute a kind of moral activity. Joan Tronto (1989) stresses that the person who is caring for another must be aware of another's needs and concerns, which may be quite different to one's own. This is no simple process for the person must at the same time have this awareness, but not to the point of either creating dependants of other people or of becoming dependent themselves, e.g. losing themselves in caring work. There is an ongoing challenge in such work to preserve boundaries between self and other. This is a problem, Tronto argues, that people must deal with constantly in all their relations with others. And yet as complex an activity as it is, caring "evokes so much of the daily stuff of women's lives" and "emphasises concrete connections with others", Tronto believes that it challenges us in to trying to define what constitutes appropriate caring and to ask why that work has been privatised and devalued in our society. In that sense, women's caring work stands as a critique of current social and political institutions. This is precisely where the work of maintaining family and the possible links between that and building community life begin to have political potential.

WOMEN AND AGENCY IN THE NORTH INNER CITY

This current study follows on from previous in-depth studies of women in the inner city, in which they revealed their competence in identifying what needed to change in their lives.

In a Master's thesis, Emer Coveney and Sheila Sheridan (1996) explored the lives of older mothers and daughters, who between them had seen almost seven decades of life in the inner city. They were clearly able to identify sources of oppression in their lives, like the role overload of working-class women, doing full-time physically demanding work outside the home, as well as their full-time work as mothers and homemakers. They also witnessed the importance of the extended community that was part of the north inner city. Although women had limited ways to take control of their own lives and to resist the heavy social oppression to which they were subject, they did not see themselves as completely powerless and certainly not as victims. They questioned the social system and they questioned social practices. Frequently they chose to alter the custom of keeping silent about unacceptable issues.

In another Master's thesis, carried out in the inner city on mothers' perceptions of community needs and resources, Clarke (1990) found a great awareness of women's links to one another through the extended family. This core part of one's life was an advantage. There was still a lot of the older pattern of relying on neighbours as a resource for food and other household items, e.g. to borrow a bottle of milk. There was also still a reliance on neighbours to keep an eye on younger children while they were out playing. But these levels of co-operation differed from one micro-community of flats to another. And Clarke documented women's increasing anxieties about criminal activities and attempts to establish meanings around crime. There were concerns about the lack of playing facilities in the area for younger children and potential pathways into crime. However, her respondents did not disclose to Clarke their concerns about the connection of crime with the heroin economy. The study was carried out in the late 1980s at a point when there was a minimal state response to heroin and Clarke, who worked through public health nurses to obtain her sample, may well have been viewed as too "official" to discuss the issue.

Both theses are interesting for revealing the dynamics and rhythms of everyday life in the locality. For no matter how difficult the scene has become, these local rhythms have not been erased. In my fieldwork notes, for example, I recorded that on any occasion when I left a meeting or interview accompanied by one or several of the women with whom I had been working, women greeted others on the street courteously and in a friendly manner, despite it often being late at night. Only once was a group of us barracked by a group of noisy teenagers; one of the women in our group turned round to them, gave out to them and that was the end of the attempt to annoy. These intervals were an indication of how open and friendly day-to-day encounters still are, despite the ravages of heroin in the area.

A critical dimension of the meetings we attended was the dynamic of women learning about possibilities for creating change and making active decisions around future directions for themselves, their families and for the community at large. This process pinpoints the potential for radical change that is evolving out of the crisis that the community has endured.

LOCATIONS AND TIMESCALES FOR FIELDWORK

Preliminary fieldwork, making contact with a range of groups and individuals in the north inner city, began in July 1998. These included people in the following roles:

- Anti-drugs community activists
- Community development officers
- Community leaders
- Drugs and family counsellors

- Eastern Health Board workers[4]
- Employment officers
- Family support workers
- Housing officers
- Information officers
- Researchers
- Residents' association workers
- Voluntary peer group support workers
- Women's development and training workers.

This resulted in 14 background interviews, of which two were taped. Fieldwork notes were written up afterwards for each of the other interviews. The team also attended a public meeting of parental support groups from the greater Dublin area.

The main part of the fieldwork ran from February 1999 to the beginning of November 1999. There were four principal sites for the main part of the fieldwork, all of these involving groups of women who were working with:

- CE schemes
- Community and youth work
- Drugs rehabilitation
- Family support
- Peer group support
- Residents' associations
- Training and self-development.

Some of their work was full-time, much of it part-time, some of it voluntary.

---

[4] These interviews were carried out before the formation of the Northern Area Health Board as part of the expanded Eastern Regional Health Authority.

As already mentioned above, the women fell into two broad categories:

- Women whose children had become heroin users
- Women who were working to improve community life in the wake of widespread heroin addiction.

Of course, many of the women whose children have become drug users are now also actively engaged in improving community life and thus belong to both categories. Equally, many of the women whose own children have escaped addiction have had experiences of heroin in their extended family, or through close friends and neighbours. In that sense, no woman was untouched. But those whose children were directly involved perhaps have special urgency and poignancy in their accounts as a result of their experiences.

We were not successful in making contact with women who are currently dealing with their own heroin addiction and are also coping on a day-to-day basis with the work of mothering and child-rearing.[5] However, it should be stated that, based on a previous study, where we did interview women in this situation (Coveney, et al., 1999), this is an especially vulnerable group in need of very special support and care.

The research team met with two groups, by agreement, some 15 times over a period of 10 months. Fieldwork notes were written up from these meetings. Two other groups were interviewed twice each. There were also seven individual interviews and four group interviews which were taped. In all, 29 women contributed to the main part of the fieldwork.

Chapters Three through Six will show that, within Dublin's north inner city, many women have extended the skills and decision-making they have learned as mothers to other women in crisis, and to the larger community. It is the core argument of this report that without this resource, the community would be facing even more profound dilemmas than it does.

---

[5] One participant had been very actively involved with a range of other drugs, especially ecstasy, but admitted that "heroin frightened me" and never touched it.

Summary of Chapter Two

♦ *People's accounts of everyday lives, collected together, help us to compare and understand better our individual experiences and also make sense of the situation of our community as a whole in a methodical way.*

♦ *This may be of special importance for women who are rearing their families in the north inner city, because of the way their lives have been fundamentally changed by the existence of widespread illegal heroin use in the community.*

♦ *In effect, women have had to rear their children through this period of deep crisis for the inner city, where heroin use collided with long-term unemployment, high levels of deprivation, and a lack of sufficient responses from government, all adding to the plight of individual families and the community as a whole.*

♦ *However, crises can bring about change for the better if we can take action by identifying our most urgent needs and the resources required to enable the community to move beyond the crisis.*

♦ *A critical resource for bringing about change is women who have coped and dealt with the problem of heroin use amongst their children and extended family and who have also organised to protect and improve community life for children and teenagers.*

♦ *The heart of this project was meeting with women, getting to know them, and gathering together their stories using written notes and tape-recordings. The women who participated in the research felt it was important for people in official positions of authority to listen very carefully to their experiences. This was because they also felt that it was important that those in positions of authority who do not live with heroin on a daily basis need to be made more aware of its full impact.*

♦ *It was the responsibility of the research team to ensure that women who participated were fully respected at all times and that there was absolute confidentiality around their participation and their stories.*

♦ *It was especially important to ensure that in writing up women's experiences, it was made very clear how the wider community, that is, the state and its statutory and voluntary agencies, has failed women in the north inner city.*

♦ *On the other hand, it was also important to make clear what hard work women have put in on behalf of their children and their families. Sara Ruddick's discussion of "maternal thinking" and the way women work strategically for their families and children was used here to illustrate (a) how important women's caring work is; (b) what its potential might be for bringing about social change at local level; and (c) how to challenge the state to support women as mothers far more comprehensively in their work.*

♦ *Patricia Kennedy's model of women's overlapping roles, once they have children, of caregiver/earner/lifegiver, is used to further explore the many tasks women participants spoke about as part of their daily lives, including community and support work stemming directly from their experiences of living in a heroin-stricken locale.*

♦ *The work of other writers on women and the family is used to argue that the state has privatised and devalued the caring work women do and that this is not acceptable. Women have had only limited ways to control aspects of their lives in the past in the inner city but there is a process of radical change taking place now stemming from women's activism in the community in response to all they have undergone.*

♦ *In bringing together their experiences and stories, the aim of this study is to make available to a wider audience an account of what women have done. It is also an objective of this study to show where substantial support for their work and community activities has been lacking and where this must now be put in place.*

♦ *The fieldwork consisted of (a) background interviews with a range of actors at local level; and (b) meetings and interviews with 29 women in four different groups in the inner city, conducted over a 10-month period.*

♦ *The following chapters will show how women in the north
inner city have extended the skills and decision-making arising from their lives as mothers to other women in crisis because of heroin, and to the larger community.*

Chapter Three

RESPONDING TO CRISIS AND CONFLICT IN THE COMMUNITY

WOMEN'S GRASSROOTS ACTIVISM

In her recent review of books on women and their experiences of motherhood, Alice Adams (1995, p. 424) writes that "women's restricted opportunities force them to engage in activism at a more grassroots level, where they act as agents of change without achieving significant institutional power". This argument deserves to be tested and will be threaded through this and remaining chapters of the report, because a critical objective of this research is to examine how women can exercise more agency over their lives and the issues which most affect the lives of their communities.

This chapter focuses on data obtained from a number of the background interviews that help to explain how the impact of heroin along with the complexities of ongoing social exclusion, has led to new areas of women's activism in the north inner city.

Women's grassroots activism has formed a logical extension of the informal ways women support one another at local level, as documented by Clarke (1990), Coveney and Sheridan (1996) and Rooney (1997), the latter in relation to working-class areas in Belfast. Child-minding, lending and borrowing small sums of money and everyday items of food, support through events like childbirth and bereavements, all form part of what Rooney rightly sees as "local organising" but which is nonetheless work that is "barely visible beyond the local sphere" (1997, p. 537). Rooney argues that the local neighbourhood has been traditionally seen by women to be their natural territory.

Of course the neighbourhood is where they are living out much of their active public lives, because they have been excluded in the past from more qualified and more highly paid formal employment, but also because the events in their lives are shared by so many other women. Thus some women in this project spoke during the interviews about "always" being involved in the community, supporting summer projects for school-aged children, for example, while other women found themselves so galvanised by the specific need to respond to the heroin crisis that they stepped across a boundary from informal networking to much more structured community work with relative ease.

Carol Coulter (1993) has written that throughout the twentieth century Irish women were well accustomed to searching out and creating different levels of response to the needs of people in their communities, especially the immediate needs of women, which inevitably involved their children. This tradition of activism, grounded in strength and self-reliance (ibid., p. 36), has found expression during the last two decades with women from poorer and more marginalised constituencies organising themselves on such issues as local action projects, education, literacy and skills training, personal development and health issues (Daly, 1989). By 1989, there were 98 local women's groups, many of them being grant-aided by the Combat Poverty Agency (ibid.). But Mary Daly pointed out that although the potential of such groups to bring about change at local level must be huge, there was no central funding for this work, despite the demand. The Department of Social Welfare took up the funding challenge, at least partially, and by 1992 there were 480 women's groups receiving funding.

O'Connor (1998, p. 77) notes that locally based women's groups were concerned with issues of poverty and marginalisation as they impacted on women and that the thrust of their work was to improve women's position in their families and within their communities. The growth of drug abuse, combined with growing unemployment in the late 1980s, "forced women to organise to deal with them" (Coulter, 1993, p. 50). Coulter quotes the example of a tenants' association which had fallen into inactivity in a west Dublin housing estate. Women subsequently met to revive the organisation and built a resource centre to deal with the problem of solvent abuse amongst younger children. Coulter argues that groups like this are now emerging because of a growing sense of disillusion with central government and established institutions which have not intervened effectively.

By contrast, women's commitment may be rooted in what Cynthia Cockburn (1998), in her study of women living and organising in communities which have been torn apart by political violence, sees as democracy in the making. She describes this work at the level of individual projects and local areas like neighbourhoods, and argues that women themselves see the vital need this work brings with it to observe and respect difference at local levels. As Cockburn puts it, what is important is to learn to "take care to listen to what a woman says about her sense of herself" and to remember "not to inflict hurt by making assumptions" about her (1998, p. 11). While Cockburn's study focused on women's work in situations where political conflict had led to organised militarised violence (e.g. Northern Ireland and Bosnia-Herzegovina), her findings about the need to understand and come to terms with difference at local level has meaning for north inner city Dublin.

Here women have spoken with other women who have been directly hurt by heroin, but have also given attention to, and developed a dialogue about, concrete programmes to address the unjust and extremely difficult social and economic issues which have engulfed them. This chapter presents data from the background interviews where the issues for discussion that came up have formed the points of departure for women's activism in the north inner city. They are controversial at times; there are acute problems of accepting difference, for example, when difference is a heroin user or a heroin dealer in the family.

SOCIAL EXCLUSION, HEROIN AND DAILY LIFE

In *Dealing with the Nightmare* (McCarthy and McCarthy, 1998, p. 53), the effects of extensive illegal heroin use on a south inner city community is described as follows:

> The community is experiencing a range of emotions: frustration, hopelessness, fear, powerlessness, and anger. The drug problem contributes to continuing marginalisation of the community, continuing the very cycle that has fostered the situation. It is extremely difficult for a community with

such high levels of social exclusion and deprivation to fight back.

In the background interviews in the north inner city, participants referred to a similar range of emotions. One health board worker said that people were "very frustrated" and expressed concern for "vulnerable families":

> *There is a very high rate of unemployment. Some of them are functionally illiterate. In some streets and blocks of flats, there is 50 per cent unemployment, usually inter-generational, families which are termed dysfunctional; there are big alcohol problems as well. Parents are often very young themselves and not very mature . . . there are quite a lot of teenage pregnancies, and they are getting younger. The sense of achievement and pride in their beautiful children is an important aspect. However, as they get older and get into mischief, frustration grows, and the parents are missing out on their own adolescence.*

The lack of sufficient social work cover and staffing for public health nurses increased these problems, with few interventions set in place for long enough to make a difference. One example quoted to me was of young single mothers with language disabilities. With diminished levels of traditional social support coming from grandmothers and family, the small children of these young women are imitating their mothers' language disabilities because they are not hearing alternative patterns of communication. This will translate into learning disabilities when they enter school.

A worker for a residents' association confirmed this range of problems, adding that early school leaving and petty theft becomes a part of the lives of many children and young adolescents. This worker cited a growing problem of inter-generational illegal drug use, commonly marijuana, with adults in their thirties using alongside their adolescent children. The worker also spoke about the way patterns of social exclusion have affected the community at quite ordinary levels. For example, there has been a lack of safe play space for younger children. Either there were insufficiently protected or enclosed spaces to begin with or, because of drug dealing and people "shooting up" heroin in the very few areas designated as play spaces, many parents were not able to let their children out to play unsupervised. With no access to a community centre, the work to build an effective residents' association and organise for action on such a vital issue also included having to overcome the hurdles of having no facilities like office space. The lack of a community or youth centre building also negatively affected the youth activities which volunteers struggled to keep going, like athletics and football. Football was and is a hugely popular activity for girls and boys and effective support could help develop this, which could act as a real magnet and an alternative to the minority activity of handbag-snatching from passing cars. But resources were lacking to fund even a proper pitch, let alone an appropriate team-playing structure and youth coaching.

A local development and training worker argued that too many women are very isolated and therefore unable to make full use of outside services. Thus, the first step is to ensure that services, like Women's Aid dealing with domestic violence, find ways to get the message across that they are there to make contact in a non-threatening way, so that familiarity will grow and in time enable women to become more confident about reaching out.[1] Another women's worker commented on the suspicion of women's groups, especially on the issues of privacy and confidentiality, and that it took time to build up confidence and to appreciate that participating in a group did not entail loose talk about other people's lives, but was about working to change local conditions.

Two other workers involved in counselling expressed concern that one of the cardinal strengths of inner city life, the extended family, actually could work against women when they first started to map out their own needs. It can be very difficult to state those needs and access help, if it is seen to expose the extended family to criticism.

FAMILY RESPONSES TO HEROIN USE

A health board social worker spoke of the inner emptiness and boredom that she perceived was the initial starting point for many

---

[1] Women's Aid is now acting as a support agency to the Community Development Programme on the issue of domestic violence.

young people becoming involved with heroin to the point of their developing serious dependency. Others mentioned a changing pattern during the 1980s: in the early to mid-1980s, heroin was the readily available hard drug on its own, when there was extremely high unemployment and no alternative way of life at all; the ecstasy and club culture of the early 1990s had created a new climate of use in which heroin became a fashionable add-on element.

One of the health board workers argued that long-term dependent drug use has not been as visible in middle-class areas because drug users there do not have to rob to the same extent in order to support their habit, and they also can avail much more readily of private treatment. In the inner city, openness was almost forced on the community because so many aspects of using, dealing and supporting a habit impinged all at once on the life of the community.

However, other workers felt that there was a long way to go before families could be more open about drug use. Family ties often made the admission of illegal heroin use problematic because one relative who might be dealing (usually on a very small scale) could be the source for another relative who was using. Yet women did not want to risk more trouble at family level by confronting the dealer. A frequent pattern existed where one family member was trying to come off drugs while another was still on them, which added to tensions. There were also problems of some family members either being intimidated by drug dealers or benefiting indirectly from dealing which made it a very difficult situation for women to handle.

At a city-wide meeting of local support groups, convened in November 1998, the problem of "stigma" was seen as one that must be overcome if women are to break the deadly sense of isolation that engulfs them when they first begin to suspect that a family member is using drugs or is involved in drug-dealing.

A worker in women's training and development felt that the issue of heroin use was there in the background for many women: as users themselves, former users, partners of users, and mothers or aunts of users but that it was never discussed at all due to the terrible sense of shame and failure that women tended to experience.

A health board counsellor in the area reported observing this sense of shame among many mothers of drug-using children and also the isolation. Alcohol abuse, which is common enough amongst older men, is more readily accepted by the community in general and it is thus almost easier for a woman to deal with if her husband is an alcoholic. It does not tend to carry the burden of personal failure for the woman to the same extent as is associated with heroin. The worker and a drugs counsellor both argued that mothers feel an acute degree of failure when the heroin user is their daughter. More so than sons, there is an expectation that young women will have more sense and not engage in such anti-social behaviour.

A special dilemma for the mother of a heroin user arises if her child, either a daughter or a son, has very small children themselves. Often, she must decide whether she can take care of her grandchildren on a part-time or even full-time basis in unpredictable circumstances. Mothers of heroin users still spend a huge amount of time in parenting activities, cooking meals and so on, for their adult children. The adult children tend to gravitate back to their original family home on an almost daily basis, and their own children frequently spend a portion of their day or even stay over with their grandparents.

The health board counsellor noted a recent pattern of women in their late twenties who had not previously engaged in a heroin habit beginning to use, imitating other women friends who were using in reaction to the daily stresses in their lives as a means of coping with long-term poverty.

It was generally acknowledged that fathers of heroin users have tended to be out on a limb. They found it far less easy to participate in group activities like family support and, perhaps, found an outlet instead by going down to the pub. However, many of the sports groups and clubs in the north inner city rely on the voluntary inputs of local men, work that one community activist argued should be more widely acknowledged than it is. These clubs could contribute to creating alternative social patterns to that of drug use for teenagers. Men also played a huge part in the anti-drugs marches of the late 1990s, assuming "leadership roles". A community worker quoted an example where, in marching on a dealer's flat, with hundreds of people involved in the march, the first ten rows of marchers were men, with women and children following behind. However, male leadership in marches represented for one drugs counsellor a symbolic example of the "glass ceiling" that women hit in the north inner city in their work as community activists; there is a cut-off line beyond which women do not gain positions of responsibility in the public sphere, despite the range of voluntary activities they initiate.

COMMUNITY RESPONSES TO HEROIN USE

Treatment options for heroin users have been expanded considerably in the last few years with both statutory and voluntary agencies looking at new initiatives. By 1997, the City Clinic, for example, was providing counselling and separate programmes for those smoking heroin. Other locally based statutory and voluntary efforts to help users were providing counselling, education programmes, alternative care, family therapy, "detox" programmes (where users are helped to wean themselves off heroin, without having to substitute methadone), drop-in centres, and practical support in training workshops. From the point of view of professional drugs workers, if someone using heroin seeks treatment, the first task is to get that person stabilised with methadone or "detoxed". But as one community worker pointed out, the failure rate in treatment programmes is colossal, because almost all users take drugs again at some point. Many working in the locality saw this pattern of relapse as directly related to the lack of extensive residential and aftercare programmes.

It was openly stated that without the community drugs marches which took place from the summer of 1996 onwards, the expansion in treatment options which has taken place would not have happened.

Voluntary sector and statutory sector workers alike thought that the street campaign against drugs and the formation of anti-drugs groups from the summer of 1996 had great political force which directly resulted in a change in public policy. Of all the changes in government and statutory responses to the drugs problem, most notable was the establishment of the National Drugs Strategy Team and the local drugs task forces. In the north inner city, this work built on the already existing foundations of the Inter-Agency Drugs Project, which was a community initiative, as mentioned above. The official acceptance of the policy of "harm reduction", however, continued to generate mixed reactions in communities where anti-drugs activists argued that the resources should be made available for drug-free approaches to treatment.[2]

One anti-drug activist saw the anti-drugs street campaign work as successful and argued, along with a community worker, that it brought in people from localities where there was little established community development, helping to break their isolation and acting as a catalyst for other expressions of community action.

A health board worker expressed concern that women's voices were largely silenced during some of the early public meetings on drugs. For example, some people dismissed women who spoke out about treatment issues, and about the plight of grandmothers looking after grandchildren whose parents were users and whose presence in their homes exposed these women to the possibility of eviction.

But in some local areas, during and after the marches, where there had been hardcore drugs problems with numbers of drug dealers and, as a result, a great deal of unease and even fear, women began initiatives like summer projects for the younger children to provide a counter to the drugs culture and managed to negotiate some support from Dublin Corporation for their activities.

CHANGES TO THE HOUSING ACT AND EVICTIONS FOR ANTI-SOCIAL BEHAVIOUR

In 1997, the Housing (Miscellaneous Provisions) Act was passed in the Dáil, permitting local authorities to act against tenants exhibiting anti-social behaviour by serving them with an "excluding order". This provision, which, if carried through, would require a court ruling on the eviction of an offending tenant, was meant to prevent the use of local authority houses and flats by proven drug dealers to carry out their dealing.

---

[2] Harm reduction policies refer to measures such as methadone maintenance clinics, where heroin users can replace their dependence on heroin with a stable dosage of methadone which is administered orally under strict supervision. This can help a heroin user break away from the illegal drug-dealing scene and a reliance on unsafe drug sources. Similarly, the provision of clean needles for intravenous heroin users enables them to inject themselves more safely, and lowers the risk of their using needles already contaminated with HIV or the Hepatitis C virus.

For the anti-drugs activists, this was an important measure by the government. The activists argue that it was vital to move the problem of drug dealing on from their immediate area. They knew that moving dealers on meant that the problem of dealing moved with such people to another area, but they also argued that it was then up to anti-drugs groups in other areas to cope with dealers who moved in: "that is up to the area where they go to".

One activist argued that his group was in close contact with Dublin Corporation and that as a result of such liaison, nobody with a history of drug-dealing would be re-housed in the area. Moreover, activists felt they could contact groups elsewhere to check on the credentials of someone new moving into the area to see if there was any history of drug-dealing.

Whatever was claimed about the value of clearing alleged "pushers" out of the area by many of the activists, there were hesitations about marching on the homes of heroin users, their partners and their families, demanding that they leave the area because of their involvement with dealing.

One local worker felt that the actions of the anti-drugs groups and the amendment on anti-social behaviour had created a climate of fear and that some mothers were caught in a very difficult position; those who had daughters or sons who were heroin users and/or dealers coming to visit them could find themselves reported for anti-social behaviour and, therefore, as having grounds for eviction under the 1997 Housing (Miscellaneous Provisions) Act. This worker expressed concern about the vagueness of a procedure where someone might be in a position to ring the Corporation and register a complaint that might begin an investigative procedure. It was argued that the entire process had created even more divisions in the area: why were some people allowed to stay without suffering complaints being lodged against them while others got letters from Dublin Corporation? A community worker argued that this process was not reliable in its implementation and feared that Dublin Corporation would not differentiate between complaints that might be malicious, complaints that might be ill-informed, and genuine complaints. Concerns were expressed about overzealous and badly informed individuals who had the potential to make this emerging policy on anti-social behaviour open to abuse.

When the issue of anti-social behaviour policies came up in discussions, there was one persistent story about a woman with young children whose partner had been a user and a dealer. Before his death, the woman had accepted responsibility for a seizure of drugs found in their flat, hoping to avoid his being sent back to prison again. But she then faced the heavy consequences of having to move out of the area.

If nothing else, the story illustrates the interwoven complexities for women, as they try to cope with their everyday lives and relationships within the already narrowed and over-strained context of poverty and social exclusion, and how heroin further complicates matters. A community worker argued that many women cannot prevent their partners from dealing drugs; they lack the personal and economic power to do so. Yet women were inadvertently suffering from the policy on anti-social behaviour. Similar stories included that of a grandmother who was caring for her grandchild and who had surrendered her tenancy rather than face any more trouble from anti-drugs groups protesting about her daughter's presence in her flat.

A housing officer commented that because these provisions became law at the very end of 1997, and because due process to obtain legal eviction takes considerable time, only a handful of people had been evicted. But this officer feared that over time what the Act would be seen to have done was to institutionalise the way more powerful voices in communities informally picked people out and isolated them as difficult tenants, rather than establishing a coherent and sensitised process of negotiation. On the other hand, an information officer based in the north inner city argued that Dublin Corporation was trying to prevent evictions from taking place as much as was possible, because if people were evicted on the grounds of anti-social behaviour they would never get back into local authority accommodation. Also, a residents' group needed to be officially recognised as a properly constituted group in order to enter into dialogue with Dublin Corporation about the suitability of new tenants in their areas. Of course, there was an awareness amongst anti-drugs groups that users are pushers and that the really big pushers tend to be beyond the reach of the local groups. But activists believed that they were caught in a no-win situation because, they argued, the Garda Síochána did too little to prevent drug dealing, and there was no route open to them to make their communities safer other than street protest and the Housing Act legislation.

Before the local elections in June 1999, there was a resurgence of direct action against pushers, with organised meetings, names being divulged and then marching on those households. I attended a women's group meeting where there was a spirited discussion about actions in the previous week where a particular micro-area had been targeted to empty it of alleged pushers. All the women in this group favoured action against the pushers because of the continuing threat heroin posed for the community as a whole and for all their families. They knew direct action can end badly and one woman recounted a story of direct action in Dublin ending in a man's death. She expressed deep unease about the potential consequences of direct action, but on the other hand was adamant that the pushers had to go and that the government was offering no alternative to secure safety for their children.

ECONOMIC ISSUES AND LOCAL EMPLOYMENT FOR WOMEN

As mentioned above, there are tensions around the black market spin-offs created by the dominant imprint of heroin on the community. This can happen in several ways.

What can be termed "retail dealing" at local level is usually to support a user's own habit (see Coveney, et al., 1999), but it can have wider ramifications and distorting effects. Habitual drug use requires a steady income in order to purchase drugs. In the north inner city, this income is often acquired through "retail dealing", that is, a user sells a small supply of drugs to raise enough money for their daily fix. That creates an impact on the community in two ways: one, by the uncontrolled exchange of money for drugs in this illegal market, and two, by the need for the purchaser to raise money for each drug purchase. This activity is also likely to be an illegal one.

Stealing money from local businesses and shops and from family members are common strategies to raise money for drugs, along with shoplifting and robbing goods (Coveney et al., 1999).When a user robs or shoplifts in order to get money for their fix, the stolen goods must then be converted into cash, by selling them, often at local level. This off-loading of stolen goods, usually at cheaper prices than shop prices, can indirectly create economic benefit in a community which has had very little opportunity to convert its entrepreneurial skills into legitimate work in recent decades. A statutory social worker commented that sympathy and family loyalties might often involve people in selling goods for family members.

But this buying and selling, and the opportunity for families living in poverty to purchase cheaper goods, creates another potential conflict for the community as a whole. Family members, if they participate in these economic spin-offs from drugs, can be judged hypocrites by anti-drugs activists and people involved in the drug scene alike, if they then object to the presence of dealers in their area.

So, the sale of drugs and these other spin-offs can be seen as very significant contributors to the black economy in the north inner city, but they are not the only factors. A community worker quoted recent studies which indicate that crime in the inner city has an overwhelmingly socio-economic basis. O'Mahoney (1998, p. 55), for example, has stated on the basis of studies of prisoners in Mountjoy that their profile is "unambiguously one of severe personal and social disadvantage". The community worker argued that the north inner city has been under severe pressure, especially in the early to mid-1990s, with drugs-created wealth being openly flaunted by dealers sending the worst possible messages to the younger teenagers about role models.

In a very different argument on role models, a drugs counsellor felt that she had seen how children respect their mothers more as a result of their participation in training and CE (community employment) schemes.[3] She saw this as providing excellent role models, for even if these opportunities had not as yet translated into jobs with a clear future, they created a different ethos for a family, giving a sense of purpose and public worth.

Others spoke of these benefits but observed that coherent training as part of CE and progression routes on from CE have not

---

[3] Community Employment schemes, funded by FÁS, have permitted many people previously unemployed or in receipt of a lone parent's allowance to acquire some work training and personal development skills.

been secured. The local economy is changing, with the opening up, for example, of construction work associated with the Dublin Docklands area. But much of that employment is not suitable for women, and the predominant pattern is still part-time unskilled work, especially for those with childcare obligations. CE schemes have been very important, improving the weekly budgets of single parents and permitting them to retain their secondary benefits of a medical card and rent allowance if they are in private rented accommodation.

On the other hand, CE schemes have not been accessible to all women who wish to avail of them. Women have lacked the basic qualifications and many had literacy problems which prevented their being considered for inclusion in a CE scheme. A women's training and development worker felt there is still an urgent need for pre-training schemes for women to build up their levels of personal confidence and to deal with literacy in a sensitive way. It was argued that a twelve-month period, rather than the six months usually allocated for a CE placement, was needed to help women become accustomed to the multiple demands of re-training in a workplace setting. It was also argued that the schemes need to be very receptive and flexible to suit the needs of individual participants. Often the initial motivation for a woman in applying for CE was the extra money, for example, and only later did the actual training take on meaning for her. Some women expressed no wish to go on to part-time or full-time employment but did seek an opportunity to enhance their personal development.

Concern was expressed by one local development worker about the government's planned social economy unit meant to help support local enterprise and businesses (see also Chapter Seven). It was feared that the proposed cutbacks in existing schemes, including CE schemes to fund the work of this unit, would have a negative impact, especially on women and on lone parents. This worker was also concerned about the demand for commercial viability of local businesses. If the social economy unit was meant to support community businesses for the first year or two only, after which they must become profit-making, this would be difficult in the north inner city, as people have low paid jobs at best and cannot afford to support profit-making business like commercially run crèches.

Accessing affordable and suitable childcare has remained a huge stumbling block for women on CE schemes, for those seeking paid employment and for those who might want to participate in schemes like the Whole-time Jobs Initiative. There simply has been insufficient subsidised childcare in the north inner city for women and these needs have not been built into any assisted employment training or work schemes.

The themes raised in these background interviews will re-emerge in Chapters Four through Six, expressed through the experiences of the principal women participants in this study.

Summary of Chapter Three

♦ *This chapter focuses on data obtained from a number of the background interviews that help to explain how the impact of heroin, along with the complexities of ongoing social exclusion, has led to new areas of women's activism in the north inner city.*

♦ *It also raises the issue that women's grassroots activism does bring about change but often without their achieving any level of power in existing institutions.*

♦ *There is, however, a strong argument that women's grassroots organisations have the potential for creating democracy at local level in a situation where many people in the community are disillusioned with central government inaction on issues that are adversely affecting their lives and the lives of their children.*

♦ *The background interviews revealed a series of problems and dilemmas for the community. Amongst those cited were:*

  o *High levels of long-term unemployment*

  o *Alcoholism*

  o *Lack of safe places for young children*

  o *Acute isolation and shame for women and families affected by heroin use*

  o *Sense of failure for mothers when they discover their children are using heroin* o *Dilemmas about caring for grandchildren for the mothers of adult heroin users with very young children*

o *Fear about exposing the extended family to public criticism or abuse due to illegal heroin use and dealing illegal drugs*

o *Concern over limited drug treatment options and the lack of aftercare*

o *Concern over the lack of preventative strategies on drugs*

o *Need for anti-drugs marches because of government inaction*

o *Concern that anti-drugs activism had created divisions in the area, with additional pressure on women as carers of children/grandchildren and/or as partners of users or people accused of dealing*

o *Concern about developing a reliable process for dealing with the anti-social behaviour that drug-pushing and dealing represent*

o *Problems created by that part of the "black economy" that centres on drugs: selling drugs; buying and selling stolen property.*

♦ *Women have tried to reach out to create new roles for themselves socially and economically as well as tending to the immediate problems created by heroin. They have continued to display a strong ethic of community voluntary effort, setting up playschemes for children in areas which have been made unsafe because of drug-dealing and drug use. They have also created family support groups and challenged their experiences of social exclusion by seeking out self-development courses and re-training options.*

♦ *As yet, however, there are very few real workplace opportunities for them to utilise newly acquired skills at a decent rate of pay. The lack of affordable childcare also remains a huge stumbling block for them.*

♦ *The themes raised in the background interviews will re-emerge in Chapters Four through Six, expressed through the experiences of the main women participants.*

Chapter Four

WOMEN AND THEIR FAMILIES

Patrice Di Quinzio (1999) points out that everyone has a stake in how mothering is organised, from the state through to individuals, all of whose needs and desires differ in relation to where they are located, politically, socially and personally. And, she argues, almost all mothers do their work to the dissatisfaction of many of the players who want a stake in mothering. Moreover, all mothers are not equally valued. Di Quinzio observes that mothering can be "delegitimated" if it takes place in less socially acceptable circumstances, and that these circumstances frequently include women who are poorer or who are seen as in some way dependent on the state. This can be a source of considerable stigma, so, for example, women who are drug users frequently suffer the judgement of outside agencies as being inadequate mothers. Yet women themselves may report positive experiences of mothering in the midst of such difficult circumstances (see, for example, Coveney et al., 1999).

If both positive and negative aspects of the experiences of motherhood are common to all women who mother, the context of these experiences can be widely different and therefore little understood by those who do not share similar stories. This is especially true of women whose children are heroin users, not least because of the sense of stigma, failure and inadequacy that women feel is visited upon them by an uncomprehending outside world. With drugs in the family, one woman explained "you become private, you draw into yourself" because the stigma is so great.

The central message that came through in the fieldwork was the extent to which women had worked hard to rear their children in extremely daunting circumstances, because that was their principal role in life. But as patterns of addiction emerged amongst sons and daughters, their mothers endured almost inexpressible anguish. When they realised there was a drug problem, women commonly went through stages of anger and denial. They were furious with their children and had "running battles" with them, often seeing their homes literally ruined by the destructive need to feed a heroin habit. One of the hardest aspects for women was to continue to be available at some level as mothers, but to accept that there was often nothing they could do for their children until their children could deal with their addiction themselves.

In the course of the fieldwork, I was introduced to a photocopied collection of poems written by recovering addicts and family members of addicts, trying to make sense of all they had undergone.[1] There are several by mothers which make clear the way this anguish rips through their lives and the extent to which the parents come to be brutally realistic about their child's circumstances, yet still hopeful that recovery is possible. In this extract from one, entitled "My Son", a woman writes:

> When I reared my son
> My worst biggest fear
> Was praying to God
> He would never take gear
>
> Now just 12 months ago
> One very cold night
> He said "Mam, I'm on gear"
> I just cried all night.

The poem goes on to recount that her son is currently in prison and that his girlfriend is pregnant, bringing home to the mother/grandmother the double importance of the need for the message that heroin can kill. But it is how she expresses her relationship with her son which deserves consideration, the fact that she has not given up on him, even though she has had to learn to draw boundaries:

---

[1] This collection has no title page nor are there authors' names for the poems I quote here. Therefore I cannot give the collection a citation in the bibliography. But I am very grateful to the individual (who will remain anonymous in this study) who introduced me to them.

We've been through some good times
We've been through some bad

But when I look at my son
He is all that I have.
At death's door he has been very near
And now I thank God
I still have him here.

In another poem entitled, "An Addict's Life", a second woman writes:

An Addict is someone
Who'll do anything for gear
He'll beg steal or borrow
Because he's the pusher to fear

An addict is human just like you and me
He's ruining his young life
But he cannot see
Most people will tell you
An addict is scum
But I can't agree 'cos I gave birth to one
I love my young addict, I know he loves me
But about his addiction we just don't agree

I pray he'll get better, I pray that he will see
That him being an addict
Is just killing me.

Here is a delicate and sophisticated assessment of the social disgrace that attaches to being a heroin user because the out-of-control addiction must be fed, no matter what it takes. At the same time, the woman can see the user as her son, hoping that he can recover, knowing that if he does not she too will pay a terrible price.

FINDING OUT ABOUT HEROIN THE HARD WAY

When first finding out about heroin use in the family, the word "devastated" seemed to speak for every woman's reaction:

Well I had a child on drugs and when I first found out he was on drugs I was devastated and I didn't know where to turn.

Despite the fact that life in the inner city has been permanently marred by heroin and by the way of life that accompanies it, knowledge about the drug can remain curiously distant until women discover that their children are using. Below is an account of an aunt who must come to terms with her niece's addiction, and with the fact that she simply does not know what to do or where to go for help:

> *I was in the _____ one night with a friend of mine, and this girl came up and said, "Do you know your niece is strung out?" I didn't know what she was talking about. I hadn't got a clue, I knew nothing about drugs, I hadn't got a notion. So, I said, "What do you mean, 'strung out'?" Says she, "She's on heroin." Ah, I was devastated, 'cos she used to be always with my young one, they palled together, the two of them, the two of them was exactly the same age. So I didn't say nothing, so the next morning I went over about nine o'clock to my sister's house. Me sister didn't even know either. I said, "I don't know what's going on, but a girl told me and I'm just telling you, you know, to sort it out or whatever." So, she was in her room, the young one, and I went and I was sitting in the bedroom, talking. Her eyes was black, circles around them, and I said to her, "I just want to ask you a question, are you taking drugs?" "No, I'm not, no I'm not, I don't know who's saying that, everyone is saying that." . . . And with that she started crying and I said, "You are." The minute she started crying, I said, "You are." So she said, "Oh, what am I going to do, what am I going to do?" So, I didn't know where to go or what to do.*

Not only are women uncertain about what to do, it is often hard to speak to anyone even in their own family about it, which increases their personal isolation and sense of burden:

> *The child that's taking drugs, it's not only him that's affected, or her, it's the whole family, it affects the whole family and relatives and everything, like, everyone gets involved in it, you know. I know when it happened I couldn't talk to anyone, my family didn't even know, like me sisters and me brothers and that, none of them ever*

> *knew. It was only when he went away for the first time
> that I told them.*

The woman below describes vividly the range of emotions that
women can go through in the early stages of coming to terms with
a child on heroin:

> *He was on it for a while before I even knew he was on it.
> But like that too, when you find out, it's an awful shock.
> Then you go in to denial, you don't want to know about it,
> you turn your back on it thinking it'll go away. And then
> when you realise that it's not going to go away, that it's
> going to be there and something had to be done about it.
> So, I tried to help him, and it wasn't working, so then I had
> to try and help meself, because if I didn't help meself, I
> wouldn't've been able to help him, so I was the one that
> needed help as well.*

Denial was a common theme that emerged in a meeting held in a
city centre hotel in November 1998, to facilitate the coming together of a number of family support groups already established in
many local communities in the greater Dublin area. Indeed, it was
as if the move to seek out a support group was the end of denial
and the beginning of trying to find a coping strategy for the
woman herself and for her family.

The denial of a heroin problem is almost certainly accentuated
by the social stigma of heroin, the fact that your child is classed as
a "junkie" and will not be given a second chance, as two women
explain:

> *Most of the community and people won't give them a
> chance. Once you're on drugs you're always labelled, I
> think, even if you're clean a long, long time, they'll always
> say "Ah yeah, sure he was a junkie, he was a junkie, like." I
> mean alcoholism is worse, they say is worse than the drug
> thing. Nobody talks about the alcohol, but I mean, you're
> not tarred with the same stick.*

> *No, when an alcoholic gets clean they're put on a pedestal,
> but if a junkie gets clean, they're still put down and down
> and down. They never get back, their lives never come
> back.*

In an initial session with one group of women in November 1998, a number of women in that group spoke from the personal experience of dealing with alcoholic husbands or partners, either currently or in the past, in addition to their dealing with children or relatives who were heroin users. Yet they felt that there was far less stigma attached to alcohol, despite its deeply negative impact on their lives — fracturing marriages and subjecting them to huge financial problems when money went on "drink" rather than vital household necessities.[2] One woman argued that the family culture in the inner city has been a pattern where men hand over some of their wages or their dole money (or all of it and get some pocket money back), and then go to the pub, while women take care of the families and do the housekeeping. Times could be very hard for women with an alcoholic husband. But at least women could be more open about the resulting problems, borrowing money from family members or friends if the drinking created a shortfall. They could vent their anger about their husbands with other women and also have a laugh about their mutual problems, or when men made fools of themselves while drunk. They suggested that perhaps it was easier because "anyone can take drink", whereas the illicit nature of heroin use puts the latter in a different and altogether more complex category as a social activity. They did not comment on the apparent contradiction of sanctioning what at times can amount to legal substance abuse while fearing heroin use. Instead, what came to the fore was how hard it was for women to admit that their children were using drugs.

One woman, who was interviewed alongside her husband, had the charge of denial about their child's drug use laid firmly at her feet, demonstrating the extreme levels of family tension which heroin use creates. As stated by her husband:

> *She denied it. He set up rows between me and her to suit*
> *himself, played one of us off against the other. He robbed*
> *her blind. I blame her. She was too soft on him. I told him I*
> *would break every bone in his body. I'm in debt now over*

---

[2] The issue of heroin use in a wider context of substance abuse, including widespread alcoholism and prescription drugs is one that agencies working in the inner city have expressed deep concern about for some time, especially in relation to the acceptability of "legalised" substance abuse.

> *his robbing. He came and robbed everything I had out of*
> *the wardrobe. He'd take the money out of me jacket pocket.*

His wife described how the discovery of her son's situation sapped her of all her strength and self-respect for a period:

> *Myself personally, I was going round like a zombie. I was*
> *passing people on the streets without speaking, but now I*
> *can hold my head up high and say "Well I'm not the only*
> *one," and before I thought I was the only one.*

CARRYING ON WITH FAMILY LIFE

Once women have accepted that they have a heroin problem in the family, they must absorb a new range of experiences and activities into their working lives as mothers, in effect normalising the abnormal.[3]

Fieldwork notes recount many of the situations that have now become part of the norm in women's lives because of heroin. For example, some adult children, especially sons, are in prison, usually on theft and robbery charges related to the need to support their drug habit. But when they are released, they have to wait, often for three weeks and longer, for their dole to come through. Mothers point out the illogicality of this situation for, if these young people have been locked up for robbing, depriving them of any money whatsoever for weeks after their release is very likely to drive them back to their former social patterns. Parents try to support them until the social welfare system can organise to pay them again, but this puts a strain on mothers coping with an already over-stretched budget.

One woman's son came out of prison "clean" but became so depressed, without either money or paid employment, that he returned to heroin use within two weeks, still waiting for his social welfare payment. His mother eventually got his dole in a lump sum, but by that time felt she must hide it lest her son spend it on

---

[3] Bourgois (1997: 35) has also commented on how local residents use what he terms a "normalising" strategy" to deal with the illegal drugs culture, although in the case of the *barrios* of East Harlem in New York City, they are asked to accommodate the shock of extensive street brutality.

heroin. She relented and gave him half the money to purchase new clothing, but when he failed to return that day, she was convinced that he had used it for drugs. He did return empty-handed the following day, with an account of events she was later able to corroborate with the Gardai. Her son had visited an acquaintance's house which was also visited by the Gardai. They impounded the money on suspicion of drug dealing and only when the boy's mother produced social welfare receipts, was there an undertaking that the money would be returned to her son.

Young men and women who are active heroin users are in and out of the parental home, sometimes living on the streets. For one mother, the shocks she faced were cumulative in this regard; she had an adult child who was living rough and in "a dreadful way", covered with scabs and filthy dirty. An overdose with prescription drugs and a collapse led to the child's being brought back to the family home where the mother had to bathe and tend to the child before putting her to bed.

Interviewing in one woman's home, I asked about the family photographs I saw on a shelf. The woman explained in deep sadness that the small girl in the photograph was her granddaughter but that when she was born, her drug-using father (this woman's drug-using son) was told to keep away from the hospital by the mother of the child who was not a heroin user. Her son is now with someone new who is a user. This woman has four other children and for her, almost the worst part of living with heroin has been her inability — as she perceives it — to stretch far enough for all her children because of her efforts to help her son:

> _____ took all my time when I should have been there for them. He was clean for three year up to last year. It's an awful thing to say but I've become a stronger person through _____ being an addict. You get stronger.

Her son has tried to kill himself on several occasions. She feels she is lucky because he did not succeed and gradually she has learned neither to deny his problems nor to be overwhelmed by them. She hopes that she can now be there for the rest of her family in a way that she was not for a long period, because she has set boundaries on her involvement with her son's drug-taking. She is still there for him but she is no longer swamped by his life as a heroin-user.

One of the aspects which is so hard for parents to accept is that heroin users can seek treatment but relapse dozens or even hundreds of times before they become stable and each of those instances means they run the risk of an adverse reaction like an overdose which can end in their death. Thus, everyone's expectations in the community, and realistically, amongst mothers themselves, are that being "clean" is not a permanent state:

> *People are waiting, constantly, they're waiting on them, because there is no resources out there for them, so people are constantly waiting on them to fall in their place again. I mean you're waiting yourself on it, you're waiting yourself on them to fall. You don't know when they're going to come in out of their face, or when they're going to go up to the bathroom and fall down the stairs out of their face, you don't know.*

The pressure is such that women going about their daily activities are always to some extent overshadowed by their fears:

> *It's always in the back of my mind, you know, is my kids alright? And it wouldn't be, you know, I don't worry about the eighteen-year old because I know he's at work and he's fine. I'd worry about him maybe having an accident coming home, but I'd never have to worry the way I have to worry about the other two. And they're women, they're twenty-four and twenty-five, but I still have to worry about them, because you don't know what's going to happen. You can be sitting here, and get a knock at the door, five minutes after, one of your kids is in the [hospital] after OD'ing⁴, they're dead, you don't know. Your life is on a string, your life and your family's lives, that's the way life is. It shouldn't be like that but it's the way it is, yeah, it's hard.*

Fieldwork notes from one background meeting included the following account from a woman who still has young children at

---

⁴ OD'ing means over-dosing. For an account of this, see below in this chapter.

home. Her husband is unemployed and she works daily at two separate part-time jobs, back to back, to try and make ends meet. Generally, she is up between half-six and seven a.m. to do her own household chores, make breakfast for the younger children as well as preparing them a dinner which they will have later on in the day, and then get them ready for school, before she goes off to her first job at 8.30 a.m. Her second-eldest child, a girl, has been a heroin user for the past six years. She and her boyfriend attend a methadone maintenance clinic but she expects to be able to leave her baby off with her mother, or stay in her mother's house when she needs to do so. Her mother had come home from work the previous evening to find the house "upside down". Her daughter and boyfriend had spent the day watching videos and smoking marijuana, but not watching the 14-month old baby, as they were too strung out. The baby had mashed food and sweets, including her younger son's favourite toffee pops, into the carpet, smeared them on the doors and scattered them all over the bottom half of the house without any effective supervision from the young parents. The woman was especially upset for her younger son, because she had found the sweets at a special price at a shop in town. She scrubbed and scrubbed that night to restore order to the house, knowing that she could not guarantee that the same thing would not happen the following day. She had, she recounted, two "Roche Tens" (Valium) in the house and was sorely tempted to take them and just blot out the burden she was carrying.

Another woman who is now working outside the home and is also part of a second-chance education and training programme described the burden of "not knowing" for her:

> *You leave in the morning and they're fine, they're probably asleep or they're probably having a cup of tea with you, they're planning on looking at the telly. When you get home, you don't know whether they're going to be dead in their bedroom, or gone off to get a fix, you don't know, so how can you go to, you know, work and study and that.*

Women reported having to be constantly on the alert, ensuring, for example, that money was kept separate out of harm's way, but also that the household contained no prescription drugs in any amount which could attract a user, either for themselves or for sale:

> *Even at home, in the house, you don't know whether the kids are going to get a buzz out of that or not. And they could be, and you wouldn't know. I don't have tablets around now to be honest with you, since I found out the kids are on drugs. The thing is now that you have to watch what you're getting, you know, in to the house. Anything that the kids could take out of the house, they will, and you wouldn't know about it.*

One woman concluded:

> *It's very hard for the mothers too, they want to go out and try and get on with their lives, better theirselves, what- ever. It's very hard for them, 'cos they're trying to study and do things and all that's in their minds is their kids at home and are they going to be there when they get home, are they going to be clean still, are they going to be alive.*

HUSBANDS AND FATHERS

In one of the background interviews before the main phase of the fieldwork commenced, it was suggested by a worker in a local in- ner city project that women in the inner city have a more rigid pa- triarchal family setting to deal with compared with women in the newer housing estates. This is due in no small part to the fact that where a women marries into a family in the inner city, very many of the wider family circle still live locally. Heroin and issues around heroin use and dealing can be complicated by this close family proximity. So, for example, mothers of children who were drug users found it difficult to object to male relatives who were dealing in heroin, as these mothers did not want to make trouble in the family. The marches which began in 1996 further accentu- ated the difficulty for members of the same extended family who found themselves on opposing sides of the heroin problem, as we shall see in Chapter Five. Yet what became a more male activity — taking direct action on the streets — was at the beginning, domi- nated by women:

*There was more women down here that marched than
there was men. Where the men should have been out doing
it, because they're their kids too.*

Women noted a tendency towards adult male dependency on
them and the reality that a type of near lone parenthood marks the
lives of many women because they must rear their children almost
single-handedly, while caring for a partner or husband as well.
Thus, for example, one woman spoke about how she has had difficulty convincing her husband that it is unacceptable for him to
give her only 15 pounds from his dole money for his board and
keep each week, just because that is the sum of money she accepts
from her adult daughter who is a heroin user in treatment. What is
also interesting about this story is that the woman is doing all the
work of housekeeping, bill-paying, and financial planning, in addition to odd jobs, all of which are vital to keep the family going.

Women see themselves as the doers for the family inside and
outside the home. Most of the women interviewed for this project
have part-time jobs or have worked in Community Employment
schemes, as well as being active volunteers in their community,
whereas their husbands are more likely to be unemployed, and
indeed to have been part of a long-term unemployed population.
This has led to tremendous strains for men: often feelings of personal inadequacy have ended in men sustaining a problematic relationship with alcohol. Some women reported marital breakdown
as a result of their husbands' alcoholism. One woman had largely
reared her family on her own, accepting her husband back into the
family home only when he had ceased to drink.

This next woman, who lost her brother to heroin, had a father
who was alcoholic:

*Since me brother died, he's been brilliant. He's making up
for all the lost time, he was an alcoholic. So that was terrible, I don't know how me ma lived with him for so long. He
wasn't a violent alcoholic, just one of these alcoholics that
will come in, drink every day, have an argument with
someone, just a verbal, with someone, and go to bed, sleep
it off. Then you'd be tentative, waking up, waiting to see
what humour he was in getting up. One of those kind of alcoholics. He's still the same, but we can just handle him a*

lot more. And he's a lot more involved with the grandchildren than he would have been with us. Making up for lost time they didn't have with their kids you see.

Younger women, whose husbands or partners are part of the heroin scene, also have had decisions to make about continuing a life together where there is a pattern of addiction. This woman spoke at length about her decision to break up with her partner, a heroin user, because of the effect of the heroin lifestyle on her and on her children:

The fella that I was pregnant for on the second child, he was put into prison, and I decided I didn't like him. I didn't like what I was after being living with. Because I found out he was on heroin, and I didn't know that, and that frightened me. And when the second baby was born, he was all jittery, and I'm, like, to the doctor, "How can that be, I didn't touch anything like that?" He was like, "It doesn't matter whether you touch it or not, the father was affected by it, so the child will be." And I'm like, "Even after ten months in the womb?" "Oh, yeah, the child will still be affected." So that frightened me. Then, I was going out to visit him in prison and I was like, "This is not the life for me, I don't want this life." You know, even though I had two children for him, I didn't want him. I was actually relieved when he was put into prison, I was like, "Yes, freedom." Not freedom to go out and run amok, just peace, just peace, away from it all.

Gradually, then, a pattern of what Ruddick (1990) terms "absent fathers" is emerging in the inner city, as some women learn how to define their own needs, moving into training and development work, and those of their children, and doing this separately to their partners' needs. Yet this is not to suggest that there were no supportive relationships between husbands and wives amongst the women who were interviewed, nor that constructive dialogue about children's well-being in the face of heroin addiction does not take place between partners in a marriage or a relationship.

In this vein, one woman recounted how she and her husband disagreed over the actions of their younger teenage child who had been drinking in a nearby pub. The child had readily admitted to doing so, but each parent saw it differently, influenced in part by the fact that their eldest child is a heroin user. The father's reaction was to roar at the younger child that under-aged drinking was a one-way route that would eventually take in heroin. But the woman had intervened, pointing out that the husband had done his share of under-aged cider drinking out of doors when he was a teenager and that the child was perfectly above board with his parents about the visit to the pub:

> *At least he's the honesty to tell me out straight what he's been doing.*

She and her woman friends argued strongly that a pint in a pub posed far less danger than hanging around on a street corner smoking hash, that the latter illegal route posed dangers that got all of the young ones in to trouble, if they could not be dissuaded from such activities. For her what mattered was maintaining open communication with her child. But that position may well be one that has been strengthened by her awareness in self-development work, which as yet has been taken up by very few men in the community:

> *You see the men kind of don't want to get involved. I feel that the men don't want to get involved, and in regard to the drug scene I think that the women are the stronger half. Oh they [men] might get out there and march, you know, on the drug marches you get them out there in their droves, but I mean, personally, to go to the meetings, to go to support groups and that, they don't want to get involved.*

However, on a more optimistic note, women with adult children commented that there is a shift in the inner city amongst many young fathers, who are more involved with their children, and are willing to push babies down the street in prams or to play with older children, and not think of it as women's work only.

COPING WITH CHILDREN IN TREATMENT

In *Prevalence, Profiles and Policy: A case study of drug use in inner city Dublin,* for which this project was the follow-on, it was pointed out that the range of programmes available for heroin users is related in part to an attempt by support agencies to match a drug user's changing needs as their relationship with the drug changes. So harm reduction policies include needle exchange programmes for the injecting user, while stabilisation and "detox" programmes are there to support the user who wishes to come off heroin (Coveney et al., 1999). However, treatment programmes are less likely to succeed if they do not have the support of a range of other initiatives. Furthermore, programmes and agencies need to be able to provide a consistent hands-on effort for all stages, whether it is to see a user through the early stages of a "detox" programme or whether their remit is to provide the long-term support and personal development training which are necessary to achieve a lasting sense of stability, a process which can take a very long time.

To the onlooker, there appears to be an almost fatal mismatch at times between the heroin user's complex and frequently contradictory needs and the availability of drug support services where there are sufficient resources to see the user through as an individual person with their own crises, weaknesses and potential strengths. A further complication is the social context in the inner city, where so many users live, which itself is saturated by the way of life that accompanies heroin. Dangerous though it is, this is a young people's game. Just under 70 per cent of all drug users in the inner city surveyed in the previous study were between 15 and 29 years of age (Coveney et al., 1999). Thus, one person's decision to separate from the drug means taking on the difficult challenge of redrawing their social geography, trying to isolate out and avoid the company where heroin is still a constant. Such a decision is also hedged with all the additional constraints that accompany impoverished inner city communities where disadvantage, exclusion and deep-rooted inequalities have been part of everyday life.

The previous study to this one also revealed that the most sought-after treatment by users, residential "detox" programmes, were the most difficult to access because of the high costs and few beds allocated to them, resulting in long waiting lists. The attraction of such programmes for the user is an immediate and enforced break from the drug and from the social context where it is usually found. But without long-term support, a "detox" programme of itself is unlikely to be sufficient to help a person to re-build their life:

> *There isn't any point in going away for two weeks, three weeks, three months even, even six months, and coming back with nothing at the end, there has to be something.*

Parents live through the hope and despair of treatment possibilities, almost as helpless onlookers, and one of the skills that women must learn is to step back with their own hopes, while still offering support during whatever treatment options exist or are taken up by their children. Hope that is repeatedly dashed becomes a constant reality check:

> *The same as when _____ came out of _____, sure he went straight back on gear that night, he was out that afternoon, back on it.*

> *I keep saying they have to hit rock bottom but I think even if they hit rock bottom, they're still going to do it again*

One woman gave this assessment of her son:

> *He's been away three times in detox units and it didn't do any good. But he's on the methadone programme now, but he still uses on and off, he's still dabbling.*

In the judgement of these women, the problem with many of the treatment programmes is the lack of aftercare, support and focus in the lives of users:

> *They need programmes for after they get out of prison, and recovery and aftercare, and for when they come out of the hospitals, and anywhere else they're after going for three or four weeks. That does them no good unless they have aftercare and recovery when they get out 'cos they've nowhere to go and they're hitting the streets and they're full of drugs again.*

> *They're coming home and they're left in their rooms wasted.*

There's no way for them, and that's how they go back two hours later, because when they come out of prison, there should be some kind of place where they can go and talk to somebody or, even with people like theirselves that's trying to stay clean. But there's not, there's only NA meetings, and NA meetings doesn't appeal to some of the kids, or adults, because there's people in the NA meetings that's there so long and think they own them, and they think they run them. And so the other kids won't go because they feel they're not part of it, it takes years to be part of it.[5]

A special focus of concern amongst some women who were interviewed was the nature of methadone programmes which were seen as an inadequate long-term solution to their children's needs:

It [methadone] helps them function, it helps them to live as near a normal life as possible. They can work when they're taking methadone, they can live a normal life when they're taking methadone, but it's not the answer, they can't take methadone for the rest of their life.

The methadone is a crutch, they should do something about that as well as the heroin problem but they're not doing anything about anything anyway, by the looks of it. Our kids is still the same way.

There was an acceptance that methadone in the context of a good stabilisation programme did help some people put their lives back together again but it was rejected as an across-the-board strategy by a woman who is now involved in drugs education programmes. She identifies the real problem as learning how to live a normal life and a normal routine:

I don't like methadone, I don't think it's the right approach. Certainly, for someone on maintenance, that's on it years and years, and they're actually getting their life together. But I don't believe in methadone as a long-term solution. Certainly, to detox, that's it. And if it could be a short de-

---

[5] AA meetings refer to those held by the Alcoholics Anonymous network; NA refers to the group known as Narcotics Anonymous which operates in a similar way.

tox. It's the counselling and the aftercare, that's what they need. Because, I mean, the detox is only the first stage, that's the easy part. It's getting back into a normal life and living without the buzz, you know, it's all that.

One woman spoke of her daughter's long-term involvement with a methadone programme in Dublin, where she felt that a lack of communication between staff and her daughter held her daughter back as much as the treatment itself. Her daughter had indicated that she wanted to be gradually withdrawn from methadone but felt she was making no progress towards this goal. Eventually she left Dublin and sought treatment elsewhere in Ireland:

I mean, she's crying out for help this long, long time. I mean I said this last year, she was begging them down there to take her down off the methadone, and they wouldn't take her off it. And then they told her, her metha-done was reduced, that she was coming down and coming down, and then all of a sudden she had to get, eh, a letter stating how much methadone she was on, for the doctor in _____ that she was attending with her liver and that, and suddenly she reads the letter and she discovers that she's on forty mls. and she believing that they're, you know, giv-ing her a blind detox, that sickened her altogether, so she stopped coming. But down there now, I have to say, the difference in the way they treat them, they're really really looking after her, I mean they're doing everything they can for her down there, and they're going to help her get off the methadone.

In the judgement of some mothers with children in treatment, methadone affects young adults differently and it may leave users no closer to resolving their problems of drug use in the context of their daily lives:

It makes one person, you know, very sleepy, and relaxed, too relaxed for my liking, and poor people that have kids and all, they don't want to be like that, they want to be able to get up, and look after them, and take them to the park or whatever, and they can't because they're too tired after taking it. And yet there's others that take it and it makes them hyper, you know what I mean, they're full of

*life. But, I mean, they should just know what to give peo-
ple. I think some of the people they're giving too much to
and that's what has them the way they are, and they don't
give a damn, 'cos once they go out that door of the clinic,
they don't care what happens to them, they might get run
over by a bus, they don't care.*

As the dialogue (below) between several women indicates, the decision to expand methadone programmes as the principal treatment service for heroin users was judged by some women to be
one of political expediency, a response to the drugs marches by
policy-makers who did not have to live in the midst of communities torn apart by heroin:

*They [politicians] don't have people demonstrating outside
their doorstep, d'you know what I mean? Give them
methadone, keep them happy, keep the numbers up.*

I mean they're supposed to be experienced down there.

*If they [users on a methadone programme] see a counsel-
lor once every three weeks they're very very lucky. Once
every three weeks, once a month, now come on, if that
doesn't tell you a story, what does.*

*This is it, but what have the kids got? We [women in sup-
port groups] have better, at the end of the day we have
each other, what have the kids got? And none of us have
experience, none of us have the experience to help one another but we're doing it. But we've learned from our own
experience of it, and we've learned from one another.*

*They're playing a numbers game. See they have to have a
steady number to keep them clinics open and they're playing the numbers game.*

Some women have helped their children with "detoxing" at home,
believing that this was the most effective way to help their children. One woman described this process in detail. Having first got
advice from someone local who knew about drugs and "detoxing",
she set out to help her niece:

I kept her here for six weeks and I detoxed her, but it was, I had to keep sending the kids after her, you know, if she went to the shop or if she said she was going to her ma's, you had to keep following her. The hardest part was her coming down. I was measuring it, making sure she was getting the proper dose. Say you start off with, say, eighty mls, [of physeptone] whatever, say in a week go down to fifty, sixty, then down, down, and she used to be shivering and she used to be sweating, and she used to be crying and she used to be, she didn't know whether she was coming or going, the young one. Literally. And vomiting. I'd be often in bed and sometimes I was afraid to go asleep in case she'd sneak out or something. But I used to bolt the door and bring the key in to the room with me. Lock the door from the inside and you can't get out unless I open the door. But I'd be in bed and I'd hear her in the toilet, vomiting, because everything was going through the withdrawals. But she got through it, and she thanks me for it. She was only a baby. But that's what killed me, 'cos there was only her and her ma there, you know what I mean, the two of them, and she didn't know what to do, now. No more than I did, but I said we'd find a way, we'll fix it, we'll try in any case. And I was glad, 'cos I think she wouldn't have got help at that stage, she'd have just went on and on, she just wouldn't have cared, you know. So, she was glad then, that it all did happen the way that it happened. But I said, "I don't want any thanks, I don't want to see you ending up the way half of the young ones is today, and the young fellas." She's grand now, she has a baby and she's settled with her fella.

This woman managed to source locally the methadone she used to help her niece undertake a detoxification, although she required advice on how to use it. But she was determined to bring her niece through this ordeal and to do so at once, without having to register at a clinic and risk the problem of waiting lists or to wait for her niece to get clean which she believed was required by some formal treatment programmes.

Three women spoke of going out and searching the streets for methadone for their children, of going into debt until the end of the week when dole money came through, and then paying off

what they owed for the methadone. At £15 a bottle what they pur-
chased was not cheap for someone living on social welfare, but
given their lack of confidence in the clinics, this seemed an alternative worth trying.[6]

YOUNGER CHILDREN AND TEACHING THEM ABOUT DRUGS

For women with younger children, ranging from toddlers to pre-
teenagers, rearing them now requires a constant sense of vigilance
because of the way the heroin culture spills over onto the streets.
If the children can be kept literally within shouting distance of
their homes, say on the inner perimeter of a flats complex, there is
some sense of safety:

> *Our children play in the courtyard, which is safe, it is*
> *fairly safe. It's fairly safe, the courtyard, for young kids.*
> *There's a few walkways out, there's only one way in and*
> *out for cars. You teach the kids, you sit down with them till*
> *they've learned that they can't go out the gate, they can't*
> *go out the arch. There is one family that's after moving in*
> *a while ago and their cars are whizzing in and out, and*
> *we're trying to do something about that. But apart from*
> *that, it's usually fairly safe in the flats. To stop joyriding,*
> *there's only one entrance and exit.*

But once more, women are left with the task of making normal
what is abnormal. For one thing, the actual resources for play are
very meagre. Dublin Corporation has failed over many years to
renew play structures in their flats complexes and neighbourhood
playgrounds were closed down as they became meeting places for
heroin users:

---

[6] An issue which did not come up in the course of the fieldwork was children who
might have contracted HIV or Hepatitis C as a result of their drug use. Clearly
this is an area where women might require even more support. A recent research
study for Cáirde, the voluntary agency offering support to those with HIV, exam-
ines the implications for families of living with and caring for someone who is
diagnosed with the virus. See A. O'Gorman (1999), *No Room for Complacency:*
Families, Communities and HIV.

There's nothing. There is just a courtyard and washing lines. They make swings out of poles on the washing lines. There was a slide when I moved in twelve years ago, there was a slide when I moved into _____. The slide was down in the end block, the big swings were in the middle block. We are actually waiting for precinct improvements to be done. That's what it's called. Isn't that very posh now? And we have put in for a play area for the children. But we put in for one that can be fenced off and locked at night, because otherwise it would be wrecked. We want it surfaced. It's going on a long time, we actually must get on about that.

Fairview Park, where there has been a maintained playspace, is not considered safe by parents in the Ballybough and East Wall areas unless they accompany their children there and back again.

One parent who chaperones her children at all points outside their flats complex spoke of her concerns now that her children are getting somewhat older. As soon as her eldest child leaves primary school, this mother is aware that she will no longer be able to escort her child to and from school as she has done up to now. The overriding concern is that children will drift towards a crowd with anti-social habits that would predispose them to ex- perimentation with drugs.

So it is also important to instil a sense of responsibility in even young children. A mother of four children discussed this:

I've no high expectations for me kids, I push them to do their best all the time. I mean, if me daughter wants to be a stripper, she can be a stripper, but be her best at it. Be their best, just to be their best. I mean, if me son wants to be a mechanic, well, I'll help him every step of the way, you know, whatever he wants to do. But I will not have them sitting around doing nothing. That's one thing I won't. I mean, even now they get up and they make their beds in the morning. The dinner table is like a revolver, you know, the four-year-old tidies off the table, the eleven-year-old washes the dishes, the seven-year-old dries them, the five- year-old puts them away. And that's every day, and that's without fail. Every now and again, we'll have a game of "house", you know the cards, and whoever wins gets off

*the dishes for the next day. "Please play 'house' tonight, I
want to win, I want to win." You know, if they're going
somewhere and they want to be off the dishes tonight,
"Please play 'house', please play 'house'." But I teach them
that they have to work for what they want. It's not just
gimme, gimme, gimme, and I'll give, I don't. It's like, well,
you take half and I'll give you the other half. And that's the
way I'll work it with them.*

Women ensure that their younger children are aware of the heroin
problem to the extent of cautioning them about what they must
not play with or pick up:

*Well, mine is only young, my eldest is eight, so the only
things I tell them is don't pick needles up off the ground
and they know not to. Like, the youngest, the little fella
started school, he's four, and he's always calling me a
junkie: "You're on drugs", like. And he doesn't understand
what it means, just hearing people.*

*If they went to pick a drink up off the street, that could be
phy [physeptone], it could be anything and they could be
drinking it.*

At the same time, there is concern not to take more from children
than one has to in order to protect them, given what they have already seen of the drugs problem:

*Yeah, I think you'd be afraid to say anything, just to pro-
tect her, keep her innocence for another bit longer. I know
it's probably silly, but you know, especially what she's
seen. Like, she saw the marches, Jesus, they frightened her.
We were at the window and one of them came around, and
the child was asleep in bed and she got up and she hid behind the sofa. She was terrified. You know, just with the
noise of the people coming down around. You know, so
you just want to try to protect them for another bit longer.*

But if parents are more aware of the drugs problem, this has not
necessarily translated to teaching about drugs outside the home to
help reinforce parental positions. One woman recounted how she
had sent her child into primary school with a book on drugs and

only then did the teacher begin to do some active work on the issue with the class as a whole:

> *When she was in fourth class in school, I bought her a little book about drugs and the danger, and I sat and I read it with her. And she brought it in to school, and the teacher did broach it. But that was only when she brought the book in. That was just her teacher. Maybe had it been a different teacher, she wouldn't have broached it, you know. She did discuss it with the kids when she brought the book in. You can do your best to educate your kids, I mean I do my best, I educate, my five-year-old knows about drugs, and knows not to touch things. But there's kids that don't get taught at home. And the kids who really need it, whose parents are drug addicts. How are they ever going to learn any different if they're not taught in school?*

It would appear that drugs education has been extremely slow to be implemented in schools. There is of course also an issue of the value and content of such programmes, especially where older children are likely to know far more about drugs than their teachers, so that credibility of the latter is a huge problem (Coveney et al., 1999).

Some young children have already seen something of the heroin scene through the unavoidable experiences of cousins or other relatives. This was considered to be a helpful, if bleak education for one woman, a former ecstasy user herself, whose brother's life was ruined by heroin:

> *Well, my kids are fortunate in the way they're very streetwise, they've seen the whole drug scene with me brother. Not to me, to a certain extent, they don't know about me. When they're older I will tell them about me, like I won't go behind the door, because I mean your past always creeps up on you anyway. And I mean, you could see your son, please God I won't, in say, five or six years and he's out of his face on E, and I'm saying, "What are you doing?" And someone will say, "I don't know what she's talking about, she used to do it herself." You know what I mean? I wouldn't go behind the door, I'd say, "Yeah, I did it, listen to me, I'll tell you what it's about." But I suppose I could*

handle them on any drug, but not heroin. I don't think I could handle them on heroin. 'Cos any other drug is more psychological addiction rather than physical. And I've learnt that, I didn't know that before, I really didn't.

This next woman's children saw her dealing at first hand with bringing their cousin through a detoxification:

Now, my kids seen all that, but, in a sense I was glad they seen it because we might had often had a conversation about drugs or whatever, but they seen what they went through, so it kind of knocked it on the head for them, you know that way? My young fella, now, I'd say that given a chance he'd do it, he's that kind of a young fella, "Dare me". But tip wood, he never has.

But other women did not see that personal experience of heroin use in the family was a deterrent:

It's sad, especially when they have children in tow. Your heart would break for their kids.

They're getting younger, the kids that's doing it now, and there's nothing around here for them at all, nothing. They're laughing at it going on and they're watching them doing it and all. I hate to see what's going on now, around my kids as well.

I mean it's all very well saying, "Ah, I seen them with their brother or I seen them with their sister, they won't take it", but they are going to take it. Sure there's kids only eleven and twelve and they're smoking hash, eleven and twelve? So I mean there's no end to it, and even if they see their older brothers or sisters, aunts or uncles, whatever, my kids seen aunts and uncles buried, two of them in one year, and they still took it, they still took it. So it doesn't stop them, it doesn't matter what they see. If it's there for them, if it's there for the taking, they'll take it, 'cos they want to look part of the gang. It's peer pressure with the kids as well.

Indeed it may often feel more a question of "tipping wood" than any other active strategy that protects children.

Older Children, Drugs and Life Chances

With teenaged children, it becomes more complicated just to keep tabs on one's children, let alone to know whether messages about avoiding heroin have been absorbed. Women in one group noted how they try to keep talking to their older children about heroin, but are unsure as to the impact:

> *I just sat down and talked to her about it, and to be honest with you, I told her that if she ever came on drugs, that I'd take her own life meself, rather than let her walk around the way some of them do, so she kind of has a bit of fear there, hopefully. I will take her life, though.*

> *I think it's good to have a fear in them.*

> *I think there's a few parents, as well, that's afraid to say anything to them in case they say, "Well, she's giving me all this crap, and I'm not taking it." So, they'll go out and do it. They're afraid that they're going to turn the opposite way. Preaching to them just encourages them.*

A similar dialogue emerged in another group of women:

> *Well, we don't know if they haven't dabbled. They go out, that is the fear when they go out. When I was sixteen, seventeen, my mother didn't know. So, I don't really know, but I don't think he does. I think it's just education, I mean, he knows, he's seen the marches, he knows what it can do. Anytime I've said it to him I get, "Oh, I'm not stupid", you know all this. He probably will try something, and it'll probably be the wrong thing, but you can't watch them. I know he's not doing it at the moment, hopefully.*

> *You know he's not a drug addict, you know that for sure. But you don't know that he's never tried anything.*

> *I don't know and I probably never will know.*

> *Interviewer: Would you have talked about it openly in the house?*

> *Yeah, but he seems to think he knows it all anyway. I know we all did. So in conversation if he's going out, I know he*

drinks, and he knows I know he drinks, and if I thought he was after going one too much, I'd give out to him. He tells me he knows more, I don't know. He seems to think he knows it all.

Interviewer: What about you?

Well, being out straight with you, my attitude always was, I was on me own with _____ for seven years before I met my partner now, and my attitude was, "Well if you want to try it, we'll both do it", 'cos we've done everything together, so we'll both try it. Now, I've brought him down, I've showed him where they sold the drugs, he seen where it went on and I'm not going behind the door about it. I told him if he wants to shoplift, we'll both go and do it. And like _____'s young fella, "I'm not stupid".

My _____ would, if I said that, he definitely would. Just to show me up.

It's working for me, well, so far, well like _____, most nights of the week, I know where he is, I have to say because he's going with a little one, and I know they go out for a drink and he has his bit of work and he does his sports, so most nights of the week, I know where he is. I'm not saying he's never tried, now I know he drinks. But, apart from when he used to work around in _____, he used to have a pint after work, I knew that, but now where he is, he has to cycle home, and he has to be in by half one, and if it's past half one, that's it, the job is gone.

These exchanges with mothers of children who have not been caught up in a heroin lifestyle point to what a lottery it is as to whether children take the route into heroin use or not. The women we interviewed who have seen their children descend into heroin addiction equally tried to instil lessons about personal responsibility, to keep lines of communication open, and to emphasise the dangers of drug use. The differences may be linked to a search for a lifestyle with a different identity, one that has status and excitement, one that appears to be fulfilled by the drugs sub-culture (Coveney et al., 1999). This is a pattern for some young people which cuts across all classes. But the sub-culture has special

meanings in the inner city where marginalisation and severely restricted life chances have been the legacy visited on young people
through the decades of social and political neglect. Crucially, this
is why prevention, in the very widest sense of the word, must include long-term strategies to create enduring and worthwhile life
chances for young people.

A woman, whose son has been a heroin user for over five years
and who is now stable on methadone and working towards being
drug-free, spoke of what a difference it has made to him and to her
that he is currently in employment on a construction scheme in
the docklands area. Even though the work is temporary, he goes at
it with great energy and has purpose each day, putting on his run-
ners, as she described it, and disappearing down the road to work.
This temporary reprieve needs to be translated into permanent
trained work.

Almost all the women we interviewed had left school at a
young age, often before even attending secondary school. Their
efforts to participate in second-chance education will be discussed
in Chapter Six. Here, it is important to note how concerned they
are to encourage their children to stay on in school or to return to
school so that they can have better long-term prospects, as one
woman describes:

> Mine was going to opt out, he wanted to do an apprentice-
> ship, and he applied, and the next day he changed his
> mind, so he's staying, he has three years left to do, 'cos he's
> gone into Transition Year. He's decided he wants to do his
> Leaving, so I wanted him to do it. We had an agreement,
> he either gets an apprenticeship or he stays in school. You
> know, I didn't want him to just leave. So, he changed his
> mind, he's doing his Leaving, well, he seems to be.

But even the older children can identify for themselves the value
of school, if it works for them, as with this boy currently in fifth
year:

> Oh, yeah, he has this idea he's not going to end up in a
> dead-end job. It's great at the moment but I mean any-
> thing can go wrong. Well, I always maintain that first
> year in secondary makes or breaks them. I wanted him to

> *go to _____, he had his place in _____ but because*
> *_____ didn't do much sports, I said well, right _____ is*
> *the next. So, the agreement was he went to _____ for a*
> *year, and if his grades fell down he was getting pulled and*
> *he still had a place in _____. And I tell you, tip wood, I*
> *have never looked back from the day he went up there.*
> *Now, I was at a parent-teacher meeting today, I had nine*
> *teachers, one I'd never met before, and they all said he's*
> *pleasant to teach, well-mannered; and I said, "Well you're*
> *not at home with him!" But however. They all praised him*
> *up to the nines.*

To keep children in second-level schooling does require yet more scrimping and saving. But perhaps it can be helpful in giving a sense of identity and purpose to the older child. One woman who has two sons in second-level at the moment just about manages, with both boys working at part-time jobs:

> *But I have to say, now, _____ and _____, they both have*
> *part-time jobs and they're both still in school. But seriously*
> *for a lad to stay on, and you're trying to support a sixteen,*
> *seventeen-year-old to do their Leaving, and I find that's*
> *probably half the battle with me, like, he sort of supports*
> *himself, he's only two nights a week, and he's not hard on*
> *money, he's not really materialistic, and he's no problem to*
> *me, he's not looking for money all the time. . . . But the*
> *money for him is important, it's important that he can go*
> *to school and not have to keep getting money off me all the*
> *time. If he shouldn't be working and trying to study, it*
> *doesn't always work out, it wouldn't have worked out on*
> *him, he'd have ended up giving up.*

The woman whose son is currently in transition year described how she has tried to encourage him to remain and to sustain his motivation, even though he will be 19 when he finishes:

> *My fella will be nineteen. I think it's because I left at thir-*
> *teen I wanted him and I kept on at him. I was able to leave*
> *at thirteen easily enough, and I didn't want him leaving.*
> *Like, he's sixteen now, he could have left from January, and*
> *that was the dodgy bit, you know, hoping that he didn't just*
> *opt out. But I think it's from saying, just keep telling them if*

*they stick at it, the end is the different choices you have in
work the rest of your life, and just keep, that's what I keep
saying to him. Even when he wanted to go for the appren-
ticeship, I says, "Well, hang on and try and do your Leaving
and at the end of the day, you can do that still." Then, we
didn't get encouraged, I didn't feel we got encouraged. My
parents didn't encourage me enough, and it wasn't their
fault, I didn't want to go either. Going from primary school
on, six months and as soon as we moved, that was the opportunity, they [the school authorities] didn't know where I
lived. I left and that was it.*

Everyday Life Then

At an informal meeting one day, a group of women spoke about
their own childhoods, and all the things they used to do. Getting
sent out to Howth to collect periwinkles off the rocks and bring
them home for their mothers to cook and then selling them locally
was a strong summer memory. Picking blackberries near Spencer
Dock while trying to avoid being chased off by the security guard
was another.

But much of the conversation focused on how hard life had
been for their own mothers, how hard they had worked every day
to make ends meet. Women would have earned extra money for
the household by taking in washing, for example, as well as working outside the home. And then there were all the home duties associated with rearing usually a large family, where paid employment for the father could be uncertain. The onset of long-term illness for a woman's husband or being laid off increased the hard-
ship and pressure on the woman.

There were no romantic or nostalgic views about this era as being the "good old days". The deaths of siblings through illness or
accidents in childhood was not an uncommon experience, and
some women with whom this group had grown up, who could
have hoped to live longer than their forties or fifties are already
dead. Long-term health and associated life chances are here firmly
intertwined with social location, and the "overwhelming evidence
for persistent socio-economic influences upon health" (Blaxter,
1990, p. 5).

And yet, there were some freedoms and opportunities for children which have been completely lost over the last 15 years or more. Women recounted the playground facilities which used to be run by the Catholic Social Welfare Bureau in the 1950s and 1960s, for children up to twelve years of age:

> *We looked up to them, when we had them.*
>
> *Because they used to do the clubs, when I was in there, and they used to do the cooking.*
>
> *They learned us how to make fairy cakes!*
>
> *Rice krispie cakes and everything.*
>
> *They used to get a load going in, didn't they?*
>
> *It was like, first in, first served, you know. There was that many at the door, waiting to get in. You'd be sitting there from six o'clock until half seven.*

Here is the account of an adult woman in her late twenties of her childhood, at a time when there was a larger community involvement backed up by a city-wide investment in activities for children:

> *I'm here all me life, born and reared in _____. It was brilliant, though, when we were kids. There was everything for us, we had the Dublin Tennis Parks' League, all the kids got involved in it, we had disco dancing. Maybe I was the sporty type, I got involved in everything. There was five-a-side football for girls, there was the normal football team for girls, a Wednesday night disco, a Friday night disco, you know, and then Mondays and Tuesdays they'd have a club in the night time, then after school there was a club, and you'd go in, if you came home at three, your club would be from three to five. And you'd do different games, you know, relay racing and arts and crafts, and it was brilliant, it really was, it was always packed. . . . We used to go on weeks away from the Dublin Corporation hall, they used to organise that. When I say "away", I mean down to Oakwood, down to Killure House, down to Killnacrott House. That's away, that was away for us.*

Her account of teenaged years document phenomena which remain part of the current scene — under-aged drinking, discos, and boredom, but not heroin:

> But when we were teenagers we were hanging around corners, doing nothing, so we heard of a disco for teenagers, and it was up in the CIE hall in Marlboro Street. _____ it was called. So, we all went up, saw kids our own age, like having a few drinks before they went in, so we found a fella down here that sold flagons for three pound. So, we used put a pound each, tell our mas the disco was two pound. It was a pound in, but we'd get two pound each and buy flagons, go to the disco. Tell our mas the disco was over at one, where it'd be over at eleven, so we'd have two hours to kind of sober up, and doss around town and all. I think I was fourteen when I started going to the ____ in _____ Street. It was brilliant. The first time I went up, I'd a step in me hair and your man says, "Go home and get your nappy changed." But the following week I got me hair done, I got streaks in me hair, I got it cut tight, got me ma to put makeup and all on me, and we got in . . . But from then on, we kind of strayed out of the area, but up to then, our fellas was in the area and we used to hang around in a gang. But when we hung around in a gang, I found, we all put Indian ink on our arms, played chicken with glass, you know, daredevils. We'd sit on a roof all day, just for boredom, nothing else to do.

This woman left school at 14 years of age. On the issue of early school-leaving, another woman stated that:

> Everything was based on getting a wage then . . . I wasn't going to stay in school when I could be earning a wage.

There is a strong memory of being able to call on one another for help, a series of possibilities that was broken as re-housing took place:

> I'd a great childhood, coming up in the flats, used to always play together. Remember we used to be all on the swings and sitting out.

I think it was much better in the flats, you had more of a community and a close relationship with the people in the flats.

Everyone helped each other out.

If you'd no sugar, no milk, butter . . .

Yeah, you could go and ask for a teabag or something, but down here you couldn't . . . That all stopped as the years went on. People just feel isolated in their houses now, don't they?

The heroin culture was a far distant phenomenon:

To be honest with you, I don't remember a drug scene; whether I was too naïve or what. I can't even remember the first time I was aware of drugs, you know. I think the first time, I remember hearing about a family from the _____, that there was three of them that died from drugs, and since that, I know another two of them have died. I suppose that would be about the earliest. I remember years ago, there was Today, Tonight, *I think, or something, had a programme on about drugs and you would see somebody injecting, "Oh, that's what they do", you know, "How could they do that?" And I think it was based around Ballymun. Now, Ballymun to me was the country, you know, then. But I just wasn't aware of it, even in school. I don't remember being even told anything about drugs, or warned about drugs.*

EVERYDAY LIFE NOW

Women in inner city communities still know many of the people they see or meet, as they do the rounds of their daily shopping and messages. But social relations have been fractured by heroin.

The homes where there are heroin users living with their parents have frequently been physically destroyed by the anti-social behaviour that can accompany heroin user. And, as heroin has become a divisive issue in their community, women have often found themselves defending their flawed family member, and facing the disapproval of the wider community rather than casting them out.

But this has deeply wounded them, adding an additional burden to a daily life already complicated enough. For those who have put their children outside the door, their lives are quieter but they have to struggle very hard to accept the necessity of addressing their own needs:

> *With the daughter, my life is quieter without her being around. Well, before I was so upset about it, but now if she doesn't come home, I just say "Well, she's elsewhere," you know. But before I'd be up looking out the window waiting for her, and everything else. I don't any more, I have my sleep now. I didn't have for months with her, you know, I'd be up looking out the window and then, and minding her child at the same time, you know?*

Users continue to visit neighbours as before, but they may well bring the physical complications of heroin with them:

> *A young one I know, oh God, comes in here. She went to that _____ [drugs agency], she went everywhere, now she's still on it, but she often comes in here, and I swear to God, the sweat does be pumping out of her. She fell on the floor one night. Out. She must have only took it five or ten minutes before she came in here. I had to get her up off the ground and that's how she came back to herself. Trying to talk, couldn't talk, couldn't even talk she was that bad . . . She was off it and she went back on it, she's back on it now, you do know, 'cos when she comes in here, the way she does be talking. I don't think that she'll ever give it up, she's on it too long. She's on it a couple of year, that young one. She has a young one of six, she has another young one, I think he's four or five. Two boys. I don't think she goes off it, she does say she goes off it, then she gets heavier, then the following week she goes round. And a very nice young one. They're all nice young ones, it's just what happens to them.*

In the midst of these challenging realities, all the normal events of people's lives go on. One day, with a group of women, there was a discussion on home decorating and much interest in how to modify gas central heating systems and what to do with the fireplaces, once gas was installed. They exchanged information on where to go for materials — a balance sought and achieved between all the competing pressures that is staggering for the levels of personal stamina and courage they are required to draw on each day.

Here is a terrible day's events for one woman, which she spends in hospital with her son, after he has been delivered home to her, very ill as a result of a bad heroin fix:

> *I ended up in the _____ hospital on Thursday night with _____, after getting a bad hit. Whatever he got, he came home in an awful state. But it's even gone that they don't want to know in the hospital, you're treated like a lump of dirt that was left there, I was very sick with the flu, I couldn't talk, my temperature was sky-high . . . I looked and, a taxi pulled up, and he got out and he was like a corpse. He could hardly walk, I had to give the taxi man six pound and say "Where did you pick him up from?" "_____" he said, "he was on his own, love." I said, "Thanks very much." He said, "If you haven't got the money . . ." I said, "No, thanks, thanks very much." He said, "I wouldn't leave him," he said, says he, "I wasn't even sure I'd get paid but," he says, "I wouldn't leave him out there." Anyway, he [her son] just, he kept rubbing his hips and his legs and saying they were all gone numb, kept telling me they're gone. "I don't know what's wrong with me, I don't know what's wrong with me, me head and all." . . . And he went up to bed, and in two minutes, here's how he was in the bed [gasps] . . . his two lips were like two big plums, but his face broke out all purple and white dots and I woke him up about fifteen times in less than, say, twenty minutes. He kept saying "Will you leave me alone, I want to go asleep." The sweat was pumping out of him, he was just like a ball of fire . . . I got the ambulance, but I said to the ambulance man, "I don't know whether you're wasting your time, he took heroin ages ago." I didn't say it to him about him OD'ing last year, but I said "When I seen his face and his lips going purple," I said, says I, "That's what really worried me, and the way he was breathing." D'you know what the ambulance man says to me? He says, "Does he always tell you what he's going to do?" That is on my grandchild's life. I said, "I wish he did," I said. "He's after coming home and he couldn't hardly walk," I said, "I*

shouldn't have even been in tonight, only for I'm sick myself."

They whipped him up out of the bed anyway, and "come on, come on" and start roaring at him anyway, and he got up out of the bed and the two of them are holding him up, walking him down the stairs, out into the street with nothing on him, a T-shirt and a pair of shorts. We went in the ambulance, sure he got sick all over the place in the ambulance and all, and your man said "You were saying you might be wasting your time? You probably wouldn't have had a child in the morning," he says to me, "I'm telling you now love."

So anyway, we were brought into hospital, and I went down and I says, "Excuse me, is there any doctors on, we're here eight hours." "Yeah, there's two doctors on," but they kept going over and looking at people's files, opening them and as true as God I can nearly sit here and swear, now when they seen it was drugs-related they were putting it back to the back, because I walked out and I seen him, and he was fifth on the list, and when I went out he was eighth, and I said, "Excuse me, would you tell me what way they're coming from," I said, "He's after being down there and now he's back up here," and she kept coming over and putting me behind the curtain and pulling the curtain over. So at four o'clock in the morning, I went out and I said to the doctor, "Excuse me," I said, "Would you mind coming in and having a look at him," I said, "I'm here hours and hours, I'm here since before twelve o'clock," and I said, says I, "He seems to be coming round" . . . So anyway, she asked him a load of questions and . . . she let us go home and phone for check-ups, but he was up vomiting the whole night after . . . but, like, he slept all the time he was in the hospital, like he only woke up at about twenty-five to four in the morning. He slept, you know what I mean.

Now what I think that, when they looked and seen it was drugs, they didn't give a damn. It looks like that. That's exactly what it looked like to me. They just didn't want to know. That's what I'm saying. They're on drugs and that's

*it, you're dead. They done that to theirselves. They're the
scum of the earth, that's the way they look at it.*

Fortunate in the taxi driver who picked up her son and brought
him home, fortunate that she was ill and at home that night rather
than going out with a group of work colleagues for a special event,
this mother and her son then receive less than sympathetic treatment in hospital because of his status as a heroin user. This is the
work of being a responsible parent to a drug-using child. It is also
what stigma means and how it attaches to the drug-user's family.

> *It's the same if they don't even know they're on drugs. If
> they go up with a broken finger or a broken leg, the minute
> they hear they're on drugs, they don't want to know, just
> don't want to know. If they go in to the Rotunda to have a
> baby and they hear they're on drugs, they don't care about
> them, they treat them like shit, they treat them like kids,
> even if they're not young. They could be twenty-five and
> they could be thirty and they could be on drugs and the
> minute they find out they're on drugs, they're treated ter-
> rible, terrible. They won't tell them nothing that's going on
> about their babies, about theirselves, nothing.*

Despite all her hard work and her wishes and hopes for her children, once a woman has been forced to learn about heroin in this
way, she may feel an even greater sense of obligation to respond to
others. Here is the account of a woman, intervening on the street,
because she knows what the struggle to keep clean is for a young
adult user:

> *I was coming home the other day and there's a young fella
> in front of me, and this other fella, now I knew that the
> fella was on drugs, you know, 'cos you know the looks of
> them then, and eh, he said to this other young fella in front
> of me, "Are you lookin?" and the young fella says, "Ah no,"
> says he, "I'm trying to kick it . . . ah, another little bit won't
> harm me," and he's kind of standing there, and of course
> I'm saying "For fuck's sake, leave him alone!" Now that's
> what I said to him, and your man kept looking at me, and I
> just said, "Keep walking son, if you want to sort yourself,
> your life out," says I, "Don't mind any of them," I said. And
> you're just walking past and "Are you looking?" you know,*

"Lovely stuff . . ." you know "A little bit more heroin" . . . "I have good stuff . . ." It's not the thing, they're out there encouraging them back on to the drugs again, they've no hope at all. I mean to say, you're walking down the streets, and you know that what they're doing, they're selling, and you're walking along.

One day, walking along with one of the respondents, she and I passed a house close to her own. She gestured towards the front door and said:

Her son in there killed himself last year — he was fourteen.

What this brought home was not simply the lack of comprehensive support services for users, but the neglect of users' families. One woman argued that she would really rather be dead now than see another one of her children go through what she has already seen her eldest child endure as a heroin user and go through what she has endured herself. She expressed it this way:

I'd rather be up in heaven with them looking down on earth than go through what I've been through in the last five year.

Summary of Chapter Four

♦ *Women as mothers are important to everyone in our society. Their children and other family members, the community and the state, all have an interest in how well women do the work of child-rearing and family-building.*

♦ *However, many women can experience a sense of stigma as mothers because of their social circumstances which are unfavourable or which attract disapproval from other sections of society who have no understanding about these circumstances.*

♦ *The majority of women interviewed in this chapter are mothers of heroin users and, as a result, the women themselves have experienced an acute sense of stigma and failure in trying to come to terms with their sons and daughters. With* drugs in the family, they felt that "you become private" because the stigma of heroin use is so great.

♦ *It was common for women in the initial stages of realising that their child had developed a problem with heroin to feel terrible grief, anger, and denial. The word "devastated" was used most often to describe how women felt when they first discovered that their child was a heroin user.*

♦ *The whole family is affected when one of the children is involved with heroin, and commonly the woman was trying to stretch her energies in many different directions to give support to the heroin user, as well as care for the rest of the family.*

♦ *An important turning point for many women is when they recognise that there may be a clear limit to the help and support they can give their child as a heroin user. A woman must learn to be there for her child but at the same time to step back.*

♦ *There is great anxiety from day to day about whether their sons and daughters may experience an overdose or a relapse, if they are on methadone, or if they are "clean" altogether.*

♦ *Yet women have to continue and get on with their own lives, their work, and their own self-development, despite the heavy burden on them. This burden can often entail looking after their grandchildren, because their own children who are heroin users need extra support with very young children.*

♦ *Husbands and fathers can and do play a supporting role to the women in many instances, but women are the principal doers of family work and the problem-solvers around issues that relate to care and support for the heroin user. Many women have to adjust to a lack of consistent support from their husbands, who themselves have suffered the effects of long-term unemployment and some of whom have a history of alcohol abuse.*

♦ *There is great concern about the limited forms of treatment available to their children who are trying to deal with their addiction. Methadone maintenance is seen as "a crutch" and* not a long-term answer at all. But at the same time, they see no alternatives being widely developed for the numbers of young people in need.

♦ Mothers of younger children are working to educate and, to the extent they can, protect their children from aspects of heroin use, supervising their playtimes in public areas, teaching them not to pick up discarded syringes and so on. With older children, women rely on trying to talk with them, to warn them of the consequences of heroin use, and where possible to encourage them to remain on in school, while discouraging any activities which may lead to settings where heroin is used. Almost none of the women interviewed had received a full secondary education and now, they place a great value on education and trying to encourage their children to remain on in school.

♦ They are clear that their own mothers had very hard lives indeed but that for them as children, growing up without heroin made their childhoods easier.

♦ By contrast, daily life now, especially for the mother of a user, is filled with uncertainty and pain. Despite that, many women are working very hard to maintain their own stability and normality and that of their family.

Chapter Five

DIRECT ACTION CAMPAIGNS AGAINST DRUGS IN THE COMMUNITY

SEARCHING FOR WAYS TO PROTECT CHILDREN

There are high social costs attached to illegal drug use for individuals, families and their communities. At the level of the community, the problem is not so much with illegal drugs in and of themselves but with the negative environment they create. This is especially true of heroin or crack cocaine. To fund "hard" drug use requires cash which is obtained from activities like theft and robbery, frequently in the immediate locality, if not from the actual families of illegal drug users, from prostitution, illegal drugs courier work and very commonly, from street retailing of drugs (Bourgois, 1997; Coveney et al., 1999). Both the highly addictive nature of these "hard" drugs and the way the illegal street market works promote their circulation. On the one hand, the selling of street drugs can become a "normal" activity because their use is so common and an everyday event in certain localities. On the other hand, this very "normality" and availability help to expand the numbers of young people who become users (ibid.):

> *That's what I'm saying, it's easy money. Even half the kids, if they can get away with it, they're not going to work, if they can sell drugs they can get three weeks' wages in a day, so why should they work, when they can get it selling gear? And some of the kids is easy targets for them, that will sell, even if it's only hash, they will sell it, it could be three pound, four pound, whatever, and then what they're making out of it. It's quietened down a lot here, because it was bad now, about two year ago. Jesus, you couldn't go*

out on the street, they were on every corner, anywhere you went, and you know them 'cos they were dealing openly, they weren't even hiding it. They were just doing it. It's sad, but I wouldn't like me kids to end up like that, now. I'd go mad.

As a result, parents are deeply anxious about the need to protect their children from becoming enmeshed in the heroin sub-culture or from becoming re-involved with it. Their strategies, however, are few in number, at individual and family level and, as we have seen in the previous chapter, they may rely on no more than the hope that talking to children about drugs will discourage them, or that chance factors, like older children wanting to stay on in school or doing work they like, will help them to direct their energies towards non-harmful activities.

Collective strategies to deal with drugs, arising from within the community, were also effectively limited. This is in part to do with the extreme difficulty of dealing with an illegal and widely spread activity, but in part also reflects the lack of resources that were made available to communities over decades of official neglect. An example of this neglect is to be found in the Sean MacDermott Street area of the north inner city during the early 1980s. The Youth Employment Action Group, as we saw in Chapter One, had identified job training and work creation as crucial elements to secure an alternative future for young people.

The local community also identified the need for best quality, relevant, comprehensive second-level and third-level education to diploma level as a vital resource. Community and parish groups campaigned for the establishment of a community college, drawing up briefs, collecting statistics on local education participation and meeting with officials in the Department of Education and the VEC. Although the potential of the college as a focus for community-led development and participation was abundantly evident, its construction did not take place. Very belatedly, more than 15 years too late for the young people in the area who have since grown up with heroin, work on the college was finally begun at the end of the 1990s, and Larkin College is now actively contributing to the life and the value of the community.

Varley (1998, p. 390) presents data on community action groups in the 1990s, arguing that when community action has come "from below" rather than as a result of state initiatives or partnerships, the objective has been to mobilise a local population on an issue which appeared to threaten a community, either as a result of an external force or because of the state's inaction or misguided actions. There has been a strong emphasis on highlighting environmental issues, and also on objecting to the withdrawal of services at local level which was seen as detrimental to the community. In the case of the community college, for example, the campaigning was to obtain a resource urgently required by the community.

Anti-drugs marches comprise a different sort of direct action, an attempt to target a threat which is external, in that the large supplies of heroin come from outside the community. However, the external sources are vague and shadowy, compared with the real and constant presence of middlemen dealers and street sellers who live in the community, and it was the latter two groups who were targeted by the marches and protests.

Anti-drugs Concerned Parents marches first became a strong community response in many local Dublin areas in 1983, when heroin addiction had already reached crisis point. Local and national news print and media stories regularly referred to the groups as "vigilantes", whereas the groups adhered to the perspective that they were responsible parents, highlighting a threat to their lives and families in which the state appeared to have no interest. These two conflicting definitions of the marchers' intent remain finely balanced in the descriptions of the marches which re-emerged in force during the summer of 1996.

Curtin and Varley (1997) have discussed the tendency of community action responses to be either oppositional in orientation, where groups at community level see the state as problematic and needing to be challenged, or integrationist, where the emphasis is on building partnerships, with the state giving the lead in resources to help encourage communities to deal with job creation and so on at local level. The community has recently emerged as "a significant actor in policy discourse" in respect of economic initiatives which it has been in the state's interest to pursue (ibid., p. 382), albeit with problems around the sustainability of local-level partnerships. Yet for the state to respond to the drugs issue and to transfer its emerging models of partnership to the social context of widespread drug use required a direct challenge from the communities themselves.

North inner city communities have consistently made the case, from the early 1980s onwards, that drugs prevention strategies must respond to the social and economic context of heroin use. A serious and focused co-ordination of prevention and treatment services was one of the objectives of ICON, at its formal establishment in 1992, and of its Inter-Agency Drugs Project (ICON, 1999, p. 13). A second objective, the support of local tenants' groups in conducting street marches and public campaigns to draw attention to the open dealing in the north inner city, had successes like the Action Day in October 1995, attracting over 1,000 people in protest, and the setting up of the Dublin CityWide Drugs Crisis Campaign, which launched its first policy document in May 1996 (ibid., p. 14).

But it was not until the publication of the First Ministerial Task Force Report in 1996 that the state finally began to seriously engage with arguments about the need for extensive resourcing at community level to aid community development as a strategy in prevention. There is no question that the marches and the circumstances of journalist Veronica Guerin's murder contributed in a major way to this change of direction.

Many of the anti-drugs marches were at the sharp end of collective community action on drugs and were caught up in the problems that Varley (1998) identified as occurring with autonomous community action, including problems of minority participation and a small elitist leadership. However, the marches were also a manifestation of the acute frustration felt in a locality where people had worked with absolutely minimal resources for many years to try to build effective prevention, treatment and support strategies at local level. And, periodically, the marches have continued to take place.

In Chapter Three, I discussed the group meeting where women were debating the resurgence of direct marches against drug sellers or pushers who lived in one north inner city locality. The orchestrated approach of a public meeting, where names of the people to be marched on that night were drawn from a hat, bore all the hallmarks of elitist control. Nonetheless, Special Garda actions like Operation Dochas,[1] to arrest dealers, including street dealers, were never seen as sustained or effective enough to change the situation. This view would be strongly reinforced by encounters like that described in Chapter Four, where a young person trying to remain heroin-free is approached on the street by a drug seller. Thus, many women viewed the potential of the marches to drive out local drug-dealing as a pragmatic move, even if the retail sellers went elsewhere or the marches achieved only a temporary respite locally.

WOMEN, MARCHERS AND DIRECT ACTION

The motivation for women to accept, lend approval to, participate in, or even initiate marches, was bound up with the immediate welfare of their own children, nieces and nephews and so on:

> *You blame them sellers, they're sitting back, they don't take it, but they kill some other one's child with it, do you know what I mean? It's all right for them to earn a living out of it, but then there's no mother at the other end of it, or child being on it, do you know what I mean?*

This concern brought a gendered dimension to the marches and their organisation, where women as carers and mothers were making known their needs. However, it was a position fraught with tension:

> *Well, it wrecked the community.*

> *Well, even when all them marches was on, going back, now, that was what? Four year ago now, there was too many families involved in it in the first place. So, people was getting out marching and they were fighting with one another, you couldn't go in the pub, you couldn't go in the shop without getting called inhuman names. But people that was getting out was doing it for their own kids, not*

---

[1] This was a special once-off operation by the Garda to clear drug dealing from O'Connell Street and the immediate area around it in 1997.

*for anybody else. People that was out doing it, was doing it
for their own. To try and stop it.*

One younger mother chose to help the community by networking
with information on drug users needing treatment resources and
on unknown people who were possibly dealers moving into the
area. Below, she identifies, as a mother herself, with those of her
own generation who have died and those left with their burdens,
to explain why community action was so critical:

> *The generation I am from there are few of them left alive.
> They are either dead from an overdose, dead from other
> drug-related difficulties, strung out, on and off the clinic or
> else coping with living with the virus. There are so many
> grannies living around here rearing two and three daugh-
> ters' children, some grannies not necessarily around here
> rearing gangs of kids . . . The biggest thing for me was
> when my youngest was going to school in _____, and I
> would walk up and down every day and I would see all
> these pushers selling — '93, '94, '95. They were openly sell-
> ing. Now they never asked me because they knew I wasn't
> interested. Others were asked. I used to get so fucking an-
> gry — "I'm not leaving my child around here to end up like
> this". . . . As the drug marches started up, they [dealers]
> started moving here. Now that was getting too fucking
> close. So I started talking to friends and neighbours. And
> then the community started to become a bit more aware of
> people moving in. . . . So they set up a committee and I said
> I couldn't be involved with the committee but I would net-
> work and feed as much information as I could to and from.
> And that is exactly what we done. The community got or-
> ganised, started a few marches, put out the word that
> whatever help was needed for whoever needed it, drug in-
> formation, rehabilitation, anything at all. So if they were
> stuck with someone they didn't know how to handle, they
> could come to me and I would make the contacts and tell
> them where to go. It was all kept very anonymous and
> very well done.*

This account also highlights the value of women's informal social
networks. In general, within Irish working-class communities,
these networks are thought to be larger than those in comparable

communities in England and elsewhere, and are strongly related to large family size and kinship networks (Leonard, 1997, p. 113). The emergence of a strong informal sector of women's community development groups has undoubtedly benefited from those larger social networks. Women's informal networks had a positive impact on the marches themselves insofar as women had a strong presence on marches in many localities in the north inner city:

> *There was more so women than there was men.*

> *There was a big meeting in the _____. Then they started marching. The meeting went on for two or three weeks, then they started marching up to the doors, and they were outside protesting all night. Staying out all night and all. But there was more women than there was men.*

> *The whole community, well don't get me wrong, the whole community didn't stick together, but the best part, the majority of them was women. And they stayed together, right up to the very end of it.*

> *Interviewer: And were any of you involved in the marches? Who was involved?*

> *All of us.*

> *Interviewer: What ages were your kids when you had begun to march, were they still little ones?*

> *Mine was just two.*

> *Mine were all teenagers. And then I had a granddaughter, she'd have been five. Like, I was going out doing it for all the kids, 'cos they were doing [dealing] it too openly.*

One woman related in great detail her own reaction to Veronica Guerin's murder and the subsequent determination of communities to take action:

> *I'll tell you when it started . . . Veronica Guerin was after being shot dead. And it sickened me, you know, I was in shock . . . That was July, I think, '96. And I wanted to write a letter, I wanted to do something. Prior to that in me own*

*area, I was looking at the dealers, openly dealing on the
street. There was one fella in particular, and I used to see a
queue of people up to his flat, a queue on the stairs, it was
literally like a supermarket. And I remember, I was over in
me friend's flat, she lived facing him, and her son had a
pair of binoculars. I remember taking them out one day,
and you could see him passing over the heroin, and I was
saying, "What's this all about?" And nobody was doing a
thing about it, you know. On the other hand, then, at the
next corner, you had the addicts. They were snatching
bags out of cars. Watching this every day, and them running up the stairs to the flats, and their mas looking over
the balcony, watching them doing it, the young fellas out
of their heads, obviously looking for the money for their
next fix, you know.*

*So _____ decided to hold a meeting, because they were fed
up with all the pushing that was going on, and all the crime
related to it. . . . And it was then that they decided to form
an anti-drugs committee. So they went round knocking on
doors, and said, "Look, we're meeting up at _____ at such
a time, come along if you're interested in saving your kids"
. . . So, the next week, they held a meeting and asked for
people to come forward. . . . It was new to the area, it was
new to the inner city at the time. But the whole inner city at
the time had risen up, and decided to do something about
the problem. . . . And I remember one chap in particular
telling us, the people who had gone forward, meself included, that if you weren't in it 200 per cent to leave now.
And he told people what they were faced with; that they'd
probably fall out with their brothers, their sisters, their
neighbours, and they'd be slagged off for it.*

*I was so angry I didn't care. I said, well the worst that
these people can do is kill you. The only thing I had reser-
vations about was me family, you know, the home, if anyone started messing. You know, retaliation regards the
home or whatever. But, where I was concerned, I didn't
care, you know. I was just so angry, I didn't care. And as
well as that, then, that Christmas, me cousin's young fella
died from an overdose, and he was only fifteen. That was
close to home, then.*

This woman goes on to explain how the anti-drugs group worked at local level, with meetings, putting together information on suspected dealers, organising patrols through the locality to discourage street dealing, and also trying to set up a treatment committee:

> *We got going then, and we started to meet every week. And basically, what we did at these meetings was pool all our information together: who we knew was dealing, who we knew personally was dealing, and as time went on, people were coming to us on the side, and saying, "I think he or she is dealing over there, or there's something going on over there." And there was one fella in particular where the dealing was happening from, and the committee went and hassled him, marched on him.*

> *The marches happened every one or two weeks, marching on somebody's house. This is at a local level. And you'd get anything from 100 to 160 people. It wasn't very well supported, because, like that, people were afraid to be seen marching because they'd family or neighbours on drugs. So they weren't going to put themselves on the line.*

> *So, as time went on they did fundraising, they ran raffles, and bought more sophisticated walkie-talkies, the real thing, and they were used well. As well as that, in the early stages, there was a lot of women involved. I'd say out of the twelve, probably six or seven were women. That's on the committee. But as far as patrols were concerned, you'd loads of women in the beginning. Probably more women. And it was decided that the women would patrol the area during the day. And some of the women offered to do the nights. It was a bit of crack, sitting out there. They had one of those drums, you know, for keeping them warm as the winter approached. It was a good bit of a laugh at times.*

> *As well as that you had people that got involved in the patrols for the wrong reasons. They just wanted to smash heads, you know. But they were weeded out as well. The patrols went on for a good few months. They went through the winter, the first winter, anyway. And obviously the numbers dwindled and come the end of the winter everyone got tired.*

They had a subcommittee which was supposed to look af-
ter the treatment end of it, you know. A treatment sub-
committee. I was kind of put forward onto that. During the
whole time I was on that, which was probably the guts of
two years, I think two people came forward. I felt totally
inadequate being on that committee, because I didn't know
what to do if somebody did come to me. Right, I was open,
I knew where to go for help, or where to send them, but I
still felt that that was inadequate, you know. But then,
having said that, there wasn't really much of a problem,
because, as I said, only two or so people came. And, look-
ing at it now, it was obvious why they didn't come, because
we were after being out marching on these people and
they weren't going to come to us for help. We were the
ones that were marching around, knocking on their doors,
you know what I mean?

This account points to the commitment people had over a period
of some five months to protect their locality. But it also suggests a
number of problems with the direct action approach. At least for
this woman, although she was clear that she wanted to be involved, there does not appear to have been a great sense of owner-
ship of the process. She speaks of "they", the principal organisers,
rather than "we". And there is no explanation advanced as to why
women's involvement, which was strong at the beginning, tapered
off. It would appear that sustaining direct action was too difficult,
especially if there was an ongoing threat of violence. One woman
recounted incidents where women, helping the effort by delivering
leaflets and patrolling in the locality, were verbally abused and
threatened with rape by dealers. She witnessed one explosive confrontation between patrolling activists and dealers and their ac-
quaintances. It took 25 minutes for the Garda to arrive to lend assistance and restore order.

There was also a very uneasy relationship between the anti-
drugs groups and the police, and a strong feeling locally that the
police were openly opposed to their activities:

And any time the patrollers came out, especially the men,
the guards would appear.

Moreover, it was felt that the court system "let off" known dealers who claimed to be the victims of the activists. In one instance, it was thought that a dealer had asked for police protection against the activists and feelings about him ran especially strong because he was a former heroin user:

> *He was a user who was on methadone, and he had his act fairly much together. He wasn't using the heroin but he was selling it, and he was doing fairly well out of it, and I felt that he should have known better, more than even someone that was using and selling, and somebody that never used and was selling, you know. 'Cos he'd been there and done that, you know. He was up in court and got away with [it] a few times.*

It was reported that the police themselves referred to the activists as "vigilantes". Also, they appeared not to be able to make sense of women getting involved in the marches in any role but that of being a "vigilante":

> *Me ma is real like, she'd go on all the marches, she still does, she's very vigilant, she's not a vigilante. And funny enough, for that court appearance I was telling you about, the detective came down to the house. I wasn't there and he said to me ma, "I suppose you're one of the vigilantes as well."*

MARCHING AND NOT MARCHING

There were indications that the marches and their organisation were seen by men as a source to express masculine or even machismo energies, about which women in local communities were ambivalent:

> *You'd have the committee meetings, and half the committee were women, then you had meetings within the meeting, where the women would go and the men would stay back. Or else you'd see little meetings going on over in the pub. So a few of us kicked up murder and we were told to fuck off, you know. "Youse are only women", you know that kind of way? At the end of the day, the women were the ones that wore out more shoe leather walking around, and when you look at the marches today, it's mostly women still.*

> *And it was mostly women that took the lash when it came to
> the physical stuff as well. Women were threatened and all,
> but nobody backed down from the threats.*

Over time, patrolling local streets became problematic and con-
frontations with supposed dealers led to outright conflict:

> *That's when the violence comes into it, is when they're get-
> ting found out. That's when they start getting violent, 'cos
> they couldn't handle being caught . . . So they were coming
> out in cars, trying to run people over, and all this . . .
> That's when they were getting heavy then, with people, be-
> cause they couldn't take it, getting caught and found out.
> Their money was going down because there was no way
> some of them could sell it, 'cos they were getting watched
> all the time.*

For women in one locality at least, these differences and divisions
have left them less sure of their own roles:

> *When the drug groups started up they seemed to have a
> balance of genders. But as it went on it seemed that most
> of the men who got involved were there to go on the
> marches. But when the community decided that that was
> not the approach they wanted, they [the marches] sort of
> fell by the wayside . . . There were meetings held and they
> were told that nobody with alcohol on them can go on
> these patrols . . . They [the patrols] are supposed to be tak-
> ing a stroll down the road with your neighbour and taking
> stock what is going on. They are not about going around
> with a baseball bat, because some ridiculous things were
> going on . . . so when they were told this was not accept-
> able, they fell by the wayside. So now it is left to the
> women — the committee is made up of eight women and
> three men. The women won't go to the forefront. They push
> the men to do all the interviews, take all the credit, nothing
> has changed. They deliver the leaflets, encourage people to
> take part in the marches.*

The surveillance methods have also been uneven, if not adverse, in
their impact on some of the people accused of dealing and their
children:

I used to hang around with this girl, like, I used to do drugs with her, I used to buy me drugs from her, and it was all around at that time. It was just like classmates that never got on with her, and because that girl came into drugs, she sold drugs, it wasn't even the actual selling of the drugs, it was they didn't like her, they wanted her out, end of story. They were going to stop at nothing till she left . . . And me heart did go out to her, because she's the type of girl that doesn't know when to shut her mouth. And rather than compromise, and say, "Well listen, okay, I'm going to stop, I'm sorry, I won't do it again", no, "You think it's bad now, well, wait till I go to _____ next year, wait till you see the stuff I'm going to bring in." . . . But her life went haywire . . . Her relationship went haywire, her kids went haywire. I don't mean they started running amok in the area: quite the opposite, they went very withdrawn, and it was a horrible effect to see on the kids. And I mean the kids were old enough to know who was doing what. And it was sad, it was sad. One of her children stayed in the area, the rest didn't . . . And she went to stay with her granny then . . . She was young, but she was old enough to understand, you know.

The system of handing over names for surveillance or marching was open to abuse. Either incorrect information or misinformation about suspected dealers escalated feelings of distrust locally:

There was some of them on the committee that should never have been on to the committee, you know what I mean? Because _____ wasn't dealing drugs, he used to buy hash, and smoke it. But, I was told by a person off the committee that me name was going to be mentioned in _____. So, I could go to one of the people on the committee and say that, and they were puzzled: "Who the fuck told you?" I says, "It was one of your committee members, if you've no trust in them you've no trust in nobody." And then, like that, it fell apart, after the next meeting they had, because the people on the committee couldn't be trusted with information.

There's some people that'd just put your name into a box for the fun of it. You could be living on your own with four kids, and they'd put your name in to that box for the fun of putting your name in to it.

'Cos you done something else, probably.

Or they don't like you or something like that.

Or they could have been in trouble for something else but because this drug thing was coming up they said, well then, put his fucking name in, you know. Get him out of the street or get him out of the area.

Thus, despite an ongoing, strongly felt need to challenge dealers who live locally, misgivings about the types and effects of various forms of direct action have left some disillusioned:

We have had to have on-the-spot marches to put pressure on some people who are laughing in the face of this community. They are in the paper and making a small fortune from what they are doing and we won't stand for it. A lot of old people will get out and march, old people and women. A lot of people don't like the in-your-face stuff. I'd prefer to just stand outside with a big banner and maybe put a letter in the door but I do not like the in-your-face confrontation stuff because it always ends up the most angry one wins. It leaves me with a bad taste.

Women have made and continue to make decisions about direct action. Some women reported taking their own children on the marches. In some families, women's involvement was considerable:

Me ma is very much into it, and me sister that lives in _____ as well. And I've another sister in _____, she's not on a committee now, but just attends meetings and goes on marches, that kind of thing.

But there are levels of ambiguity for many, often stemming from their close personal relationships in one of the following roles:

- Mothers or relatives of users and dealers
- Friends of users and dealers
- Mothers of younger, vulnerable children.

Thus one woman concluded that the personal ties were too comprehensive to warrant such an approach to the problem:

> *Well, I didn't go on any of the marches, 'cos it was families and friends they were marching on, to me. That's how I didn't go on them.*
>
> *Interviewer: So, was it really difficult for you then?*
>
> *It was, yeah. 'Cos I just didn't go on the marches. No one was bothering me. It would be like marching on someone I'd be going out with in the night. And I had a brother strung out.*

Another woman was very explicit about the potential for damage:

> *The way it was, it could have been me marching on me cousin, you know, because everyone is so close. I mean, you throw a stone and you're bound to hit your relative. It's extremely close. Everybody knows each other, and everybody knows each other's business. I wouldn't go into conversation, because it can be dangerous. You don't know who you're speaking to, if you say to a girl and you could be talking to her sister's boyfriend, and you wouldn't know. It's just too dangerous. Because people were marching on their families, and then they were fighting with each other: "You won't march on him, but you're marching on him." People were leaving the march for one part of their family and then joining the march again for someone that wasn't belonged to them. It was crazy. Everyone was fighting with each other. People are still not talking over it.*

There was a sense in which the marches further fractured a social fabric already damaged by drugs:

> *I think that was the hard part, marching on your friends . . . Like, you'd know all these people, you'd stand talking to them, it was just that the names was mentioned in the _____. And no one knew where you were marching to, only the people that was on the committee. When they marched, you followed them and they marched to the door, so you didn't know till you got to the person's door who you were marching on. And it was hard in that way,*

> *when you found out who you were marching on, like you*
> *could be marching on your best friend that you drink with.*

The lack of any sense of effective democratic participation and control had left communities feeling in the first place that when they voiced their concerns, their voice was not legitimated by comprehensive government action about heroin and its social consequences. But much of the anti-drugs activities replicated that same lack of democratic process. Thus decisions about who could march where or who could be on a committee were elitist rather than inclusive decisions:

> *Interviewer: How did you feel about that organisation,*
> *that only the committee would know?*
>
> *It was hard in a way because, maybe it was right that they*
> *done it that way, because if they said who they were*
> *marching on, like, it would have got over to them to say,*
> *"Right, they're marching on you tonight." You know, so*
> *maybe it was right that the committee took it upon them-*
> *selves to say who they were going to march on, and just let*
> *the people follow.*
>
> *That time then, the committee came up. Myself and me*
> *_____ was on it, 'cos he's dead against drugs, dead*
> *against them. He was on the committee, I was on the*
> *committee, all the names. . . . Then it came out that me fa-*
> *ther-in-law was selling heroin . . . So, a big explosion,*
> *"What are you doing on the committee, with your father-*
> *in-law?" And I didn't even know. I'm sitting on the com-*
> *mittee and his name comes out of the bag. Picking the*
> *names out of the hat and whatever. So, I didn't know what*
> *to do . . . and I said I had no answers, I didn't know what*
> *was going on. _____ said, "If you want to stay on the*
> *committee, it has nothing to do with you, but none of your*
> *family is supposed to be involved, you're not supposed to*
> *be on the committee." So, one thing led to another and I*
> *came off the committee, I said for their sake and for me*
> *own sake 'cos I was getting slagged off, but what could I*
> *do?*

OUTCOMES OF THE ANTI-DRUGS MARCHES

The prime objective for many women in becoming involved with the marches was to end open selling of drugs. In some areas at least, this objective was seen as having been achieved, as with these women:

The marches have stopped.

Interviewer: Have they stopped because the drug dealing has stopped?

No, it hasn't stopped. It's not as open, you won't walk down the street and see people dealing now, but there's still drugs being dealt in _____. But as you're going to the shop, it's not right in your face.

Interviewer: So, did people change their minds about the marches?

Well, if there was a march called tomorrow, I would still support it.

The committee was still there, and they were meeting maybe once every two weeks, once a month, as it was, the drugs weren't being sold openly . . . and that was a fact. Even addicts were disappearing out of the area. Now, that's not to say, it wasn't solving the problem 'cos obviously they were going somewhere else, you know.

One woman was not so certain about outcomes because not all dealers were frightened off by the marches. On the other hand, she has little confidence that the anti-social housing legislation, passed in 1997, giving local authorities the right to set eviction proceedings in motion, is actually effective:

I think they reckoned the marches did what they set out to do, and there was no need any more to march. I think, like that, if there was someone, like there was one here in particular and they marched on him for ages, and it turns out they can't even evict him, the Corporation can't evict him. And like, that is disheartening. Something got to do with

> *Courts and he has no convictions, but everyone knows he's pushing drugs. And he's kipping there.*

Many responses about the outcomes centred on how the process had enabled the community to identify potential new goals, in spite of what was a minority group involvement in the marches:

> *It drew people together as well. It was the same people on all the marches, the same people patrolled the streets, it was the same people all the time.*

> *I think there's more of a community spirit since the marches.*

> *A lot has come out of the marches for _____.*

> *You know next door, there are meetings and clubs going for kids. An awful lot came out of them. Before that, people were just going along.*

> *Plus, it got a lot of residents' associations going. It got _____, and there's stuff come out of _____. It did get a good bit to the area.*

> *There was nothing here, there was no community effort until after all the marches.*

Another woman disapproved of the marches, arguing that getting the dealers out was hard on the children in the families involved. She also identified the underlying problem of dealers working because of their heroin addiction and therefore the need for another approach:

> *I didn't agree with the method that was being used, like drugs-out. Because I didn't think that people should suffer for the sins of their children. I just believed that sort of behaviour gets out of control, and people very rarely stick with the principle. Plus the fact that most of those pushers, most of them, I'm not saying all of them, they were doing it for the currency to feed their own addiction. So, I didn't think that was the right approach.*

For this woman, the expertise she was able to impart about the treatment needs of heroin users during the period of the marches led to a new role in the community, helping to create a drugs awareness programme:

> *Myself and me sister, now, were never really involved as such in community work before that. But we kind of started being known in the area. We started speaking up and people were listening to what we were saying . . . And we were recognised as spokespeople, you know, in addiction and the young smokers and everything else. And that's when we found out about the group. _____ had approached us and said it was a drug awareness programme, and would we be interested. And we were like, "Yeah, we'd be really interested." You know? So, that's how we got to join _____. And I stuck it out and it's brilliant, I love it. I really do.*

One woman argued that, in addition to the very important outcome of the Drugs Task Force, a new focus on prevention and education was made possible by the marches:

> *The Prevention and Education came out of it. One good thing that came out of all the meetings was that smokers of heroin were actually seen to be addicts then. Before they weren't. Like they said to _____, "You're not an addict, you're only smoking, you're not an addict. You need to be injecting to be an addict." Now, he was actually clean for a week, and then he decided he needed help, and this was when they told him, "You're not an addict." So, he went out and bought heroin and injected. Then he had to give dirty urines for two weeks, which meant he had to inject for two weeks to qualify to get methadone. Which is absolutely ridiculous. Now, it's not seen to be necessary. Thank God it's not. I mean, smoking is seen to be an addiction. So, that's one good thing that I see coming out of it. And the Drugs Task Force came out of it, too.*

DUBLIN CORPORATION AND EVICTIONS

Background interviews in Chapter Three indicated disquiet over the application of the 1997 housing legislation on anti-social behaviour in local authority housing. That legislation was another direct result of the marches, with the government finally responding to the urgency of the need for some measures to combat drug dealing taking place in local authority flats and houses. But there was little confidence about this policy amongst the women who were interviewed. On the other hand, marching had succeeded in frightening some alleged dealers away for a period, although some had since returned:

> *Interviewer: So the corporation eviction doesn't really work?*
>
> *Only if you have convictions. You have to have convictions. For pushing. Or they can't evict you. So, basically, even if you know someone is pushing drugs, unless you can get them convicted, they won't be evicted.*
>
> *Interviewer: Were there people evicted from here?*
>
> *No.*
>
> *Interviewer: What about the people who were marched on?*
>
> *They left. A lot of people left of their own free will. There was a big march on _____, and it would be, say, the fella that was in _____ would be drug dealing. Well, the girl would stay with the kids and he'd go. That has happened in a few cases. But most of them are back now. Most of them who done that, who, one half of the family stayed and the other went, they're all back. And then a lot of them wouldn't actually be the tenant. It would be the girl who would be the tenant anyway. But she shouldn't have him living there under the Corporation [rules].*

Marching, then, was seen as successful, even if it had cleaned areas up only temporarily:

Ah, yeah, it was very successful, because definitely the pushing stopped in the area. A lot of them moved out. One of them even went to _____, supposedly for treatment, and he came back and he was clear. Back into the community. Another fella who wasn't using the drugs, but was selling big-time, he was told to move and he agreed to do so, because he was more respectable, he wasn't on the gear and he didn't want the marching on his family and all. And he moved out for a good few months. And when he wanted to come into the area, I thought it was hilarious, he used to come to the committee and grovel. For permission to come in. And he did everything by the book. But the poor, the ones that were using, used to be sneaking back in, you know what I mean. You know, wait till it gets dark; and they'd be seen.

The threat of applying the anti-social legislation was indiscriminate in its effects, however:

The only thing, like, I didn't agree with was there was one person put out here, and when she was put out, that was it, it stopped. And it was very unfair, like, I know she was drug-dealing, but she had three young kids as well.

One woman was quick to observe that if there had been tough government measures on anti-social behaviour and the drugs problem before it got completely out of hand, the marching would have been unnecessary. This woman and her colleagues felt that the legislation was now working:

But, if they'd had all the anti-social behaviour and all in the Corporation before then, before now, you wouldn'ta had to march on your friends, it would have been stopped. It stopped when the marches, when the names started coming out, most of them stopped. And now, like, they're great, they're working.

I think they just really needed that, didn't they?

They needed a fright.

In retrospect, the women are correct. The Corporation should have developed measures to respond to dealers living on site far sooner through comprehensive estate management policies. Given the overwhelming evidence that most street dealers are selling to support their own habits, well-coordinated and democratic links between the community, the Corporation and the Garda would have been the sensible strategy to pursue. The development of compulsory contract-based treatment programmes in lieu of prosecution would also have proved helpful (Coveney et al., 1999).

THE GARDA PRESENCE SINCE THE MARCHES

At the time of the marches, relations with the Gardaí were badly strained in many of the north inner city localities, as we have seen above. By October 1997, the *Inner City News* local newspaper reported that not only had open drug-dealing re-emerged in the north inner city, the cessation of marches and the much lower profile of the anti-drugs patrols had opened up a vacuum (*ICN*, October 1997, p. 2). Residents argued that the Gardaí would have to work very hard to put in a serious commitment to community policing if the ground gained by the anti-drugs protests was not to be altogether lost.

Views on Garda actions collected during the fieldwork period, while not as hostile as during and after that period of activism, indicated that much needed to be done to develop an inclusive policing policy on drugs that looks at all the dimensions together. Efforts at developing community policing could be built on to help achieve this:

> *Well, the guards come down here and they just keep pulling the young fellas, searching them, dragging some of them in, some of them that was never even involved in drugs, you know what I mean? Just take them off street corners, whip them in, search them and throw them back out. Even search them out there now, in front of people.*

> *The drugs are coming back into the area, but relationships with the police have improved — the community police. There are too many strangers hanging around waiting for their pushers.*

> *I don't like to see a high amount of police in the area, I think that gives a bad vibe. I think there could be better re-*

lations between the police, and again it's educating the po-
lice into the communities. The Corporation, well, I still
think the government has created these situations in these
areas by bad housing, overcrowding, lack of education,
lack of cultural pride, they've allowed the place to get run
down. So they all play a role in it. We all play a role in this.

Since the period of the fieldwork, the initiation of the Community
Policing Forum, which is actually run by a local woman, has begun
to shift community–police relations into a new and welcome
phase of development. The Forum is financed by the North Inner
City Drugs Task Force and has the objective, amongst others, of
co-ordinating a common strategy against drug-pushing between
the community and the Garda Síochána.

TURNING TO OTHER FORMS OF ACTION

Difficulties in sustaining the marches, and the range of tensions
they set up in local communities led to people falling away from
that form of organisation in some disillusionment. But the process
in itself helped many in the community to identify where their energies might best be redirected. One woman analysed the situation
as follows:

People just lost interest and there was after being so much
hassle, I mean, the _____ himself was receiving death
threats, and threats to burn down his house. And his wife
just couldn't hack it, you know . . . Dwindled off for a
while, people lost interest, and of course, because of all the
trouble over the year, it came to the stage where
neighbours were walking by you, and spitting on the
ground in front of you, that kind of thing. You know, you'd
loads of hassle, and then what was happening was in
other areas the anti-drugs activists were labelled vigilan-
tes. And in all honesty, in other areas you could see that
their tactics were just, if a person was dealing in a flat,
they went in to the flat, threw the people out physically
and just wrecked the flat so as it wasn't liveable in. As well
as that, problems that we had had with the police, we'd
overcome them, you know, and we were starting to have a
good relationship with the guards. We had started to look

into, we had been so busy getting the pushers out, we real-
ised that there was a void there, there was a vacuum, you
know. We felt that we had to provide an alternative to the
drug culture that was taking over . . . There was nowhere,
there was nothing, and so people started to focus on that,
then, and the anti-drugs bit was kind of taking a back seat
then.

The logic that lay behind anti-drugs direct action campaigns was
the argument that all drug use is harmful and must be stopped.
In the wake of the marches, and as the measures in the First Ministerial Task Force reports began to be implemented — an expansion
of treatment facilities and the establishment of local drugs task
forces — many were challenged to rethink what would comprise
realistic policies about drugs. This woman, involving herself in
drugs education work, found herself turning towards an acceptance
of the policies of harm reduction, rather than strict abstinence:

I started out with (the ideal of) a drug-free society. I don't
think that's going to happen today, I think that's a very
idealistic view; I think we're always going to have drugs.
It's the same with drink, I mean having been educated and
that and certainly doing _____, I've come to see that
drugs of some description have always been part of our
culture. It's just that people are tuned into heroin, though
it's a much more fast-moving addiction in terms of, you
know, health-wise . . . I certainly have changed, yes, I be-
lieve in harm-reduction, harm-reduction is important. I'm
not saying that we shouldn't close our mind and work to-
wards abstinence, I'm not saying that. But certainly, yeah,
I would have changed.

It appears that the direct action campaigns and the belated government responses have helped to create a public space within the
communities themselves, where different approaches to help heroin users break from their addiction can be debated. Thus, one
woman who was involved in the marches speaks of what she
thinks are the lessons learned about the need for different directions. The dealers have returned but have learned to keep a lower
profile. Therefore, for her, the emphasis must be on education and
prevention:

> *I feel that it is always going to be with us and you can even see it now, that the anti-drug movement all over had kind of dwindled a bit, and it's just rampant again. They're being more clever this time, they're not dealing on the street, they're being careful where they deal, but I just feel, personally, that walking around town . . . I don't think it's ever going to go away. I suppose that's what would steer me towards wanting to concentrate on the education/ prevention-type thing. Because if you just save one of them, you know . . .*

Another woman understands and respects the people who were driven to take up marching because of the fears in the communities. But this has not and will not stop heroin use. She argues that even if the government were pressured to legalise heroin, its use would still be problematic. Therefore there must be a "more reflective" way of responding to the needs of people using heroin:

> *An awful lot of the people are very much involved in it, you know, and part of the marches and all of that. I accepted that's how they felt. I would put my view, like. I think they felt that they were contributing something by doing that, and that's all they had to contribute, and they thought they were doing something worthwhile, yeah. And I can appreciate the fears within communities when drugs come in, like, I do appreciate that also, you know . . . I mean, I've come to see that it's always been there, people are complex, there is no one easy way. And if we could put pressure on the government and have heroin stopped, we could, we could even legalise it. But it doesn't solve the problem . . . And it's [heroin] satisfying needs within people. And we need to tap into those [needs] in a different, more reflective way.*

The question that hangs over this period of direct action is whether, if the government had responded sooner, would it have been necessary to hold the marches? These two women saw this issue differently, one stating firmly that it was the state's responsibility to have acted sooner; the other woman saw the marches as integral to a statement about their need to speak out for their community:

If the Government would have got off their arses and done something it wouldn't have been necessary to march.

I still think an awful lot of people would have taken it in to their own hands, the way they did with the marches, like to prove a point, you know, it was their community.

Both these perspectives have implications for the exercise of democratic process and the issue of empowerment which will be explored in Chapters Six and Seven. The anti-drugs marches and direct action have brought about some vitally important spin-offs for the community; however, the negative impact on individuals and families have also added to the sense of exclusion and the fracturing of the community.

Summary of Chapter Five

♦ *The negative environment that heroin creates in the community stems from the way it circulates. Users often become street sellers in order to finance their habit. An increase in local street selling contributes to increased availability, "normalising" the drug, and this has the potential of widening the number of young people who may get involved with the drug.*

♦ *In this chapter, women speak about their experiences of anti-drugs marches and direct action campaigns mounted in the north inner city from the summer of 1996 onwards as a way to try and free their communities from extensive drug-dealing at local level.*

♦ *The north inner city had been limited in the collective actions it could hope to undertake to counter the heroin sub-culture and the context which enabled it to flourish. The area as a whole had suffered extensive systemic socio-economic neglect over several decades at the time anti-drugs marches began in the summer of 1996.*

♦ *The anti-drugs marches could thus be classified as a community action taken "from below" in a situation where the community felt that the state had failed over a long period to respond to its stated needs.*

♦ *The case for tackling the context of heroin use by responding to the depressed local economy with high unemployment, early school-leaving and very few opportunities for young people, had been made by inner city groups over the previous number of years. But these issues had not been responded to by successive governments which continued to deal with heroin largely as an individual and medical problem of addiction, rather than a social problem as well. There appeared to be a reluctance to develop a model of partnership with communities to deal with the drugs issue prior to 1996.*

♦ *It was these frustrations and, for many individual women, a real fear about their children's vulnerability that led them to involve themselves in the direct action campaigns which sprang up in the summer of 1996.*

♦ *Women did not define themselves as "vigilantes" but as concerned parents, who felt that their actions might help their local communities where drug-dealing was now a commonplace everyday activity, observed by their children.*

♦ *Women were aware from the outset of the huge tensions that marching produced in their community but did not have a sense of any alternative action available to them at that time.*

♦ *Some women helped local committees with information on dealers and users in need of treatment. Others patrolled their localities by day and night to discourage dealing from taking place on street corners or in local houses or flats.*

♦ *There were more women than men involved in patrolling, distributing leaflets, and marching as well.*

♦ *However, much of the decision-making about the location of the marches appeared to be made by a small group of male leaders. There were difficulties balancing out tendencies to violent confrontation.*

♦ *Women who participated in direct action faced verbal abuse and threats from people who were said to be dealing in heroin. Other women who did not participate were often caught up in family relationships which did not permit them to take direct action against family members who were dealing in heroin.*

♦ *Only a minority of people in the local communities ever participated in the direct action campaigns and the difficulties in sustaining them, along with the increasing tensions and divisions they produced, and the impact on some of the people directly involved, led to a falling away from this form of action by the spring of 1997.*

♦ *The marches were deemed successful in that the very open drug-dealing did cease for a long period. The anti-social legislation to prevent people from dealing from local authority housing was also seen as an important outcome.*

♦ *However, it appears that the process permitted some women to re-think priorities within their community. The identified need for wide-ranging community prevention and support, including schemes for younger children and drugs education for children, young people and adults became an important focus for renewed local effort.*

♦ *Some women felt that, without the marches, the emphasis on prevention and the drugs task forces might never have arisen as part of government policy.*

♦ *Women also argued that if the government had acted far sooner, the marches would never have been necessary.*

♦ *Marches have continued sporadically to take place. Women are divided about the marches still. Although policing and police relations with the local community have improved in some areas, women argued that in the absence of an extensive and sustained shift in policing, marches may remain a necessary option, as the drug-dealing has drifted back into various locations.*

♦ *Women's personal energies have now been largely redirected into more innovative forms of community support and capacity-building to help counter heroin.*

Chapter Six

WOMEN TAKE CONTROL OF THEIR LIVES

CONFRONTING SOCIAL EXCLUSION THROUGH WOMEN'S GROUPS

All the women who participated in this research were already active participants in community-based groups, working either specifically with women's needs or for the community. All these groups were women-only groups.[1]

The groups were concentrated in the following areas:

- Self-development

- Family support

- Education and training

- Children's play facilities and youth projects

- Drugs awareness.

Some groups fulfilled a number of these functions, both for women and the community, as women gained in self-development through skills acquisition as part of their group's work. These skills were acquired formally or informally. Some women, for example, having started as volunteers in local efforts to provide play facilities for children and through the work of applying for grant aid for after-school clubs and summer projects now have considerable expertise. Other women, in drugs awareness or family support groups, have also acquired formal training through their

---

[1] One of the groups did have some male members for a brief period but then reverted to being an all-women group.

groups' efforts to enable them to be more effective in facilitation and listening. Some women have been able to access local self-development courses, often in conjunction with CE schemes, which have extended their repertoire of skills. Literacy and computer skills courses have enabled women to go on to more formal training in areas like counselling and childcare. Women's experiences of becoming active participants in group and community work are presented in this chapter against the context of restricted opportunities for women as a result of long-term social exclusion.

Many writers in recent years have pointed out that social exclusion has a gendered context. Social policy analysts estimate that as many as 300,000 Irish women live in poverty, a significant minority of them as single parents (Daly, 1993; McCashin, 1996; Barry, 1998; Nolan and Watson, 1999). Yet, where women and their families live in poverty, very often dependent on social welfare, it is evident that "women are the keepers of living standards" (Coakley, 1997, p. 192). Here also, networks of mothers, both as relatives and friends, have been central to women generating successful coping strategies for themselves and their families (ibid.). When women have sought to create change or bring together their individual experiences into community settings to pursue objectives like those discussed above, they have faced a significant lack of state support. On issues like childcare, for example, and other back-up services for the family which would help women in retraining and paid employment, or even give women a break from onerous duties in the home, this support has not been readily forthcoming (Barry, 1998; Coveney et al., 1998a; Murphy-Lawless, 2000).

Despite these handicaps, women's efforts to train and work outside the home, voluntarily or otherwise, have been a significant feature in communities suffering from social exclusion in the 1980s and 1990s. Connolly (1997) argues that these groups, disparate in their aims, share a common goal of empowerment. Their cumulative contribution to their communities is enormous. O'Connor (1998, p. 128) argues that, in areas where unemployment has run at levels of 60 to 79 per cent, "without women's (low) paid and unpaid labour, the direct and indirect costs to the economic system and the state are likely to be very high".

The findings from this chapter will highlight the validity of O'Connor's argument and the extent to which women are working against the history of social and economic neglect which has bred its own sort of fatalism in the north inner city. One woman described this fatalism from the perspective of the individual:

> *People should have higher standards for themselves, but they don't. It's all down to low self-esteem. And then you've a third generation of unemployment down here. . . . They don't have high expectations, so they wouldn't see themselves in a high paid job. . . . You're talking about changing a whole generation's thinking around education and employment.*

Local area partnerships have made a huge difference to the structured provision of resources for women (Barry, 1998). Yet this remains insufficient to judge by the experiences that follow. Critics have argued that the structures of community action and partnership have been male-dominant (Curtin and Varley, 1997, p. 400; O'Connor, 1998, p. 246). Indeed, the "glass ceiling" and the lack of real onward opportunities are still a reality for women living in communities marked by social exclusion and poverty, despite their very much increased visibility.

BUILDING SUPPORT FOR WOMEN: FAMILY SUPPORT AND SELF-DEVELOPMENT PROJECTS

In Chapter Four, women spoke about first denying the reality of their children being on heroin and then being driven by a strong sense that they should somehow be able to help their children. An important turning point that was reiterated in a number of the interviews was when women realised they could not help their child in any of the ways that they thought they could at first. Since the break with the pattern of heroin addiction was most often not possible to achieve in any way quickly or easily, they had to come to terms with this fact and with the realisation that as women and mothers, they would need help and support for themselves in order to cope.

Family support groups have been a response to many different issues at community levels, but those set up in response to heroin problems require special sensitivity because of the heavy stigma heroin attracts. In theory, such family support groups are a tremendous asset. In practice, they require great care around the issue of confidentiality:

> *Ah, they're brilliant, I think they're vital in every area, every area should have one, definitely. But, again, in _____, you can't have a support group, because you're not 100 per cent positive that it'll be confidential. It's a sad thing to say, because there is mothers out there that could really do with it, but they won't let someone else know their business, that's the end of the line. . . . To get into a certain group of mothers in the same situation would be brilliant, but they probably have conflicts of interest with, say, their son is injecting with their daughter, you know, one son is injecting with another's daughter. They'd be fighting: "That's him, he has her up to it", or "That's her, she has . . ." And there would be murder. So, things like that are very hard to work.*

They are indeed "hard to work": one woman had turned away from her involvement in building a family support group, feeling utterly betrayed by lack of confidentiality, and has since found support in the completely anonymous and traditional structure of Al-Anon (for the families of alcoholics). But for those who are fortunate enough to have a good group structure in embryo and who can go on to build that group, its benefits are incalculable:

> *So how did I get involved with the group? I heard about this support group starting up in _____, and I decided to come along, and I came along. The first couple of times I was very shy about talking and that because you kinda feel that you're the only one that has this problem. But then when you come and hear all the other people sharing, you realise that you're not the only one. So from there on I have to say I went from strength to strength. It was the best thing ever happened to me, for me meself, not for my child, but for me. We got great support in the group. Everyone sat around and everyone shared and there was a lot of tears shed, and there was a lot of laughter as well and I don't know what I ever would have done without it.*

The capacity to identify these needs, to respond to them and to do the group-building effort is in itself a considerable accomplishment, especially when, as in the case of one group, women were working from the outset with virtually no external support or resources:

> *When we started, we were all in the same boat, because it was in the early stages. I mean it was four year ago, and there was nothing, there was none of these courses going, there was none of these task forces. . . . There was nothing . . . I think it was just that the people were all in the one state of mind, and when they all started talking, it brought them all closer together, and just made them all stronger. But as I said, it was through our own doing, nobody else's.*

Confidentiality was successfully established and maintained in this group, which has a core of some eight women:

> *I hate missing it, I do look forward to coming down, to have a yap, and get it all off our chest then, you know.*

> *'Cos we can talk to one another, we can all identify with one another.*

> *I mean what's said here is not said outside, you know, we keep it all to ourselves.*

> *You're told that at the first meeting, what's said here stays here, if you can't do that, well then there isn't any point in coming. Because there isn't any point in coming if you're going to sit in the pub and talk, or meet somebody in the streets and tell them about someone else's problem. We don't do that. The only time we talk about it outside is if we meet one another. Otherwise we wouldn't talk to anyone else about it.*

This group now meets twice a week, with courses like stress management, yoga and aromatherapy, and even line dancing on one day, while the second day is left free for counselling. With some funding from the Northern Area Health Board, they have contracted people to come in and do this range of work with them but for any additional activities, they rely on their own fund-raising.

The groupwork has helped them individually to build skills and confidence which they now feel able to transmit to other groups. They have travelled across Dublin to run seminars and evenings for other communities stricken by heroin, but do so at their own expense:

> *We are a self-help support group, we're not getting any-thing from anyone else. Not that, maybe, we haven't asked, we did put in for funding and we never got it. But I mean the point is that we do need, like we would need transport if we wanted to go anywhere, we have gone, as I said, we have gone to _____, to two different places in _____, we went to the _____ area, we went over to the _____, a few places over the _____, we went to _____.*
> *I mean that was all at our own expense.*

The group organises several weekend outings during the year, for which the women save up on a weekly basis. I was present at a number of meetings held just after these occasions and they clearly had an enormously beneficial impact on women who oth-erwise face very difficult circumstances in their daily lives. Espe-cially welcome in going away was the opportunity to put these daily strains to one side, to have a meal served up to them, to have some fun. Yet the issue that has brought the women together has built a deep level of understanding which is valued above all else:

> *Well I found out that I'm able to cope with it now. I wasn't able to cope with it in the beginning, but I can cope with it now, and I know more about it. I had to educate meself in the drugs scene. I had to go to meetings, I had to find out, I had to ask people. And the best support I got was my sup-port group . . . I've talked to other people, counsellors and everything else, but I don't believe they know what they're talking about because they haven't been there. It's the group of women that have actually been there and know-ing that they're after going through the same thing and still going through the same thing, you know.*

Perhaps the most valuable coping skill the group can foster is that of stepping back from the child who is a heroin user:

> *There's things I do now that I would never have done be-*
> *fore. Before I used to say, "Ah no, sure, I wouldn't be able*
> *to do that," or "Ah, my son'll do that". But I wouldn't now.*
> *I've got stronger since I started coming to these meetings.*
> *Now I've often got him by the scruff of the neck and threw*
> *him out the door, and shut the door in his face. Now I*
> *wouldn't take what I did once take off him. So it's only*
> *through the meetings and coming down here that I have*
> *gone like that. I used to come down here in the mornings,*
> *"Oh, he didn't come home last night," and now, it's not that*
> *you don't care, you just feel stronger about it.*

The exchange of information and experiences about current drug treatments has enabled women to begin to challenge some aspects of drugs policies; one which they pinpoint is that of long-term methadone maintenance:

> *The meetings are the best 'cos you learn so much from the*
> *meetings. When I started coming to the meetings, I did be-*
> *lieve that methadone was the solution, I really did. I*
> *praised the methadone, 'cos it kept my kids right and it*
> *kept my husband right, and they were living a normal life.*
> *But now coming to the meetings and all, and hearing*
> *about others even that's on methadone, I'm kind of won-*
> *dering now, is it? They need to do something with the*
> *methadone programme.*

This group was originally much larger but parents' reliance on the methadone programme as a solution, on getting their children taken on as clients in the local clinics for methadone treatment, paradoxically reduced the group's numbers:

> *I mean, when their kids was off the drugs, went on metha-*
> *done programmes, they [the women] gave it [the group]*
> *up because they didn't think they needed it any more. But*
> *it doesn't work that way, that's not the way it works. Most*
> *of them all got strung back out again. But the women just*
> *didn't feel it worthwhile to come back.*

This insight is important, if only to recognise the burden of profound disappointment that results for a parent when a child returns to heroin use. By their very nature, these are groups where

personal needs are great. The impact of heroin addiction on the
family, the constant crises and threat of crises are what people
must live with:

> *I mean some people go home and they fucking have no
> light, no gas, you know what I mean? Why? Because their
> children's after robbing everything on them. I mean we're
> not going home to big flashy houses, we're not driving
> round in big flashy cars.*

So there was a demand from the women for recognition of the importance of family support and for a long-term commitment of
funding and skilled training to be made available:

> *Well, all we can do is go on fighting and go on trying and
> try to get stronger every day.*

> *But it's only through us, it's not through anyone else, it's
> only through us ourselves.*

> *Sure they don't even know we're here. I mean the govern-
> ment doesn't even know this group exists. They might
> know a support group exists, maybe, in one of them up-
> stage places, but I mean as regards here, the North Inners,
> they don't know we exist.*

> *But the point is that we can't get too tired to carry on, be-
> cause we still have to come here because our children,
> some of our children are still using, so we still need it. So
> we can't afford to abandon it.*

Women's groups, whether they are oriented towards family support or self-development, have helped to break a pattern of isolation that became as endemic as heroin in the north inner city. But
there is still reluctance on the part of many women to participate
in groups of any sort. In an interview with one group of women
who had done a series of self-development courses, the participants argued that:

> *People just feel isolated in their houses now.*

> *Interviewer: And you think this _____ has helped to an
> extent now, to try and overcome that?*

It helps a certain amount of people, but not a lot of people. Like, a lot of people still don't go.

Interviewer: So there may be a lot of women out there?

That's really isolated and that is really struggling, yeah.

Well, the likes of these CE schemes is after taking an awful lot of that depression out of the area as well, because there's an awful lot of young girls working that has kids and they have the kids minded. So, they're getting out for a few hours in the morning and a few hours in the evening. It's not so isolated now, with the CE schemes. And Mary Harney, she should be shot.[2]

Breaking the sense of isolation, having a sense of curiosity and rising to the challenge of something new were some of the reasons mentioned for getting involved in self-development work:

Interviewer: How did each of you get involved with the _____, here? How did that happen?

I had the little one, she's nine in December, and like that, I was sitting at home every day of the week, and one of the women said, "Come around and do a few courses", so I started coming around, and I haven't left it. They can't get rid of me now.

A CE scheme.

Most of us was never involved until there was a CE scheme.

Interviewer: Did it take a lot of courage to come?

Yeah. It did, yeah. I was stuck at the house and I'd three kids and I was by myself. So me ma said, "Get yourself over there, they'll mind the kids, and you can do a course." I said, "Jaysus, no, I'm not going in." You have to take the one step in the door, and then that's it.

---

[2] This interview was conducted just after the Tánaiste, Mary Harney, had announced that CE schemes would be cut and drastically restructured. This issue will be discussed in Chapter 7.

In the initial stages, women had done cooking and handicraft
work, literacy and maths courses before proceeding to in-depth
specialised training. But local resistance to taking the first step
remains:

> *Like, if you say to someone, "Why don't you come down,*
> *you do cooking and whatever, and the kids go in to the*
> *crèche?" "Ah no", they say, "they just sit around a table*
> *down there, talking". You know, that's what people is after*
> *hearing, that's the impression they got, that women just sit*
> *around a table having a cup of tea and gossip about other*
> *people. Like it just takes that step in the door to see is it*
> *gossip around the table or is it what they say it is.*

REDRESSING MISSED OPPORTUNITIES: EDUCATION AND TRAINING

Pat O'Connor (1998, p. 78) draws attention to the surprising fact
that, despite the very restricted nature of the Irish social structure
for women, they had much higher access to (and take-up of) education compared with women in 12 other OECD countries, from
the 1920s to the 1960s. This access was, however, almost entirely
class-related, given that until 1967 secondary education was not
free. Even when that restriction was lifted and in the several decades that followed, women from the inner city were leaving school
as soon as possible because paid work, albeit with low wages, was
needed in their families (Coveney and Sheridan, 1996).

Virtually all the women interviewed here had left school early;
older women before free second-level schooling was introduced,
and younger women before they completed the full second-level
programme with the Leaving Certificate. Thus, an important dimension of their involvement with local groups has been the
chance to build personal confidence and to begin to search out
second-chance educational opportunities. Literacy courses have
preceded or been combined with a range of training work, like a
diploma in childcare. Counselling, facilitation, parenting skills,
community development, youth work, drama, media studies, the
Higher Diploma in continuing adult education, and coursework in
drugs awareness were some of the areas women were pursuing.
Women's centres, centres for the unemployed and other commu-

nity centres, linked to the Dublin Inner City Partnership have all provided venues to start them on their way.

The women have undertaken these courses because they want to move on to skilled work and also because they want the recognition of formal qualifications for work that many of them do already in the community in a voluntary capacity. Some have gone through the Junior Certificate as mature students and are now tackling the Leaving Certificate. And of course, as can be seen in Chapter Four, they want to be able to encourage their own children to take advantage of education in ways that were not open to them at the same age:

> *I feel great 'cos I can use computers.*

> *Interviewer: Does it make a difference for your kids?*

> *I'd say it will, in the long run. I'd say now the likes of _____ and that, that's after doing their Junior Cert, like, their kids is probably proud of her, saying, "Well, me ma is after doing something." "Well, if me ma can do it, I can do it", you know.*

> *Interviewer: What do you want to try and do for yourselves, given that you've had some training now, and you hope to get more?*

> *An education, a better way of life. Just doing the best you can, really, you know.*

> *My eldest girl, she started college last week. She's grand now.*

> *There is an awful lot of kids down here is after staying on in school compared to a good few years ago, there's an awful lot going back to school.*

Much initial coursework is undertaken not just for the opportunities that this might lead to, but because it provides a very welcome break from family duties, even if women find that hard to organise. Women with younger children have one set of constraints because there is so little affordable childcare available to release them from the home for longer periods:

> *Like, I only have young kids, I suppose me life's on hold for
> the moment anyway. Now, when me kids get to a certain
> age, I'll be able to do things for meself. You know, because
> you can't go out and do certain courses, because your kids
> does have to be minded, you've got to get baby-sitters for
> them. When me kids is older, I think I'll do something,
> worthwhile stuff. Till then, I'll have to be here for them.*

The weight of family responsibilities of a different kind, where
there are teenaged or young adult children who are heroin users,
also presents a challenge. One day, a woman arrived into a group
straight from her English class, and complete with her book bag.
But this time was deliberately carved out of her caring duties in
the home and her paid work by prioritising her own needs; an example of a learned skill.

One woman, who has a child who is a heroin user, commented
on this as a continuing conflict:

> *So how can you go to work and study and enjoy it, enjoy
> getting away from it? You have to enjoy getting away. It's
> very hard. Now I'm doing Level Two in childcare, now I
> done foundation and thing, but I struggled with it, because
> it's always in the back of my mind, you know, is my kids
> alright?*

Nevertheless, where childcare has been offered alongside coursework, women have found it an additional boon to participate and
to learn in a wider frame of reference:

> *You meet different people as well, and hear about their
> stories and that, you know.*

Those who seek second-chance education face complications and
resource restrictions. The system will not search you out. You
must either search it out or rely on the connections made by local
groups to inform you of the opportunities. One woman had
worked extensively as a volunteer youth worker, organising day
trips and weekend trips away. She wanted to train in youth work
and establish herself as a fully employed youth worker. The
chance for her to apply for a sponsored diploma course came
about through a local employment scheme which had links with

one of the larger inner city organisations. If these sorts of supports are not available, it becomes much more difficult. CE schemes, for example, which can provide vital pre-training experience for women, have had limited eligibility and time-frames of only one year for many participants:

> *When your year is finished here, you have to be at least six months unemployed, six to twelve, it all depends, before you can get another course, or go for another job. And so, what do you do in the meantime if you're doing your Inter Cert, or if you need money for books? If you get two years on a scheme, you're entitled to thirty-five pound on the Labour, then, but if you claim your thirty-five pound, your rent and all goes up, and you still don't get any supplementary grants that you're entitled to. You miss out on everything. Like, I've four kids, three of them going to school, and one in the crèche, and I missed out on a back-to-school grant because I'm on the scheme. I was over by twenty-seven pound fifty. Now, I didn't mind that, I'll have the job for Christmas, but after the job, now, I'm thinking, right, I'm pregnant, if I go for the Labour, I won't get nothing off the Social Welfare then.*

Participation in second-chance education continues to be restricted by the lack of entry places into more comprehensive programmes:

> *There was one on in the _____ I'd loving to do, but I didn't get to the meeting, and it was only a certain amount of people that was took on to it. It was like a parenting course, and you go to College, and all, and you get a scholarship. I'd love to do that for the year.*

Women want further training and proper accreditation in parenting courses, childcare and youthwork courses, not least because it would equip them to work at a skilled level in their own communities and to set an example for the young people in their communities:

> *I'd like to keep up the youth working for a while, and try and get something out of it. When it's all over, when we're finished up, try to get work out of it, elsewhere.*

I mean, I have me certificate in the hall, and every time I open the door everyone can see it, and the kids are like, "What's that for?" And I'm like, "I went back to college and I got that." And I show them the photograph, "Look, that's me when I graduated." And they're like, "Oh, can I do that? That's brilliant."

SECURING PAID WORK: CE SCHEMES AND THE FIGHT FOR SKILLED EMPLOYMENT

Anne Coakley (1997), amongst others, has described how the second-class status of women in Ireland is derived from a male model of social rights and citizenship that gives the most significant social rights to those who are full-time in the labour market and fewest to those who do unpaid caring work in the home. Without qualifications, and with their family duties, many women in the inner city have relied on very low-paid unskilled work with flexible hours which could permit them to earn in addition to their unpaid family work. Cleaning work has been a mainstay:

I'm working since _____ [her child] was two and a half. Contract cleaning but different jobs, mostly in the night-time.

I do fourteen hours a week contract cleaning in the evening. I was in the mornings but I had to switch because of the kids. But the CE schemes never applied to me, because I had to go out and clean, you know, I had to go out and work, and they would have been ideal with the kids in school, to do them, but you have to be six months unemployed to get one. But they work out better, even for the three years, but once you're already in the workforce, so it never was an option for me to go on one. I couldn't afford to sign on. I'd have liked to do one, but I wouldn't have been able to do one.

This second woman states a dilemma that has faced many women about CE schemes. The requirements have been that one must be registered as unemployed for six months or more. Thus there are women who would need to forego low-waged but readily available work for a period of time, as well as signing on the Live Register to be eligible. Furthermore, if a man and his wife were unemployed, there could be only one CE slot allocated to each household so, if a woman could gain admittance to a CE scheme, her unemployed husband would have to forego his entitlement. As a result, despite the importance of CE schemes in providing a pre-training element for women who have had insufficient formal education (Coveney, et al., 1998a), many women have been excluded for a number of structural reasons. The state has consistently failed to address adequately the circumstances of married women in relation to training (Coveney et al., 1998b) and the women reflected these frustrations:

> *None of us is on CE 'cos we're all caught in some way. Not entitled.*

> *I worked for ten years, up till I had the kids, and then I remember when the youngest of them had started play-school I said I might start looking for work. I went over to FÁS, and for every one of them I was either too old — you had to be between the ages of eighteen and twenty-five — or, and here I was, "These look great", you know, I was reading them and they were all CE. Well, I really felt old when I was reading these lists, eighteen to twenty-five.*

Women who are single parents have probably fared best with CE schemes and derived the most benefit from eligibility. Secondary allowances and benefits, like rent allowance, were unaffected by CE status, while free or very highly subsidised childcare was often built into a CE scheme. The fact that childcare could cost between five and ten pounds a week only, including a hot meal — "so you've no worries about them eating when they go home, they're after having something to eat" — made it really attractive for women to participate. Women with several children of different school-going ages still faced problems of co-ordination in collecting their children from school and ensuring they were minded, but the part-time nature of CE, twenty hours a week, made even that aspect more manageable.

Some women had experiences and criticisms of schemes which were badly handled, and offered little real training:

Yeah, I'm in an organisation which provides all that, not everywhere does. You know, _____ will provide all my training for me, even when I was on a CE scheme. But not every organisation. I've spoken to other colleagues who were doing CE schemes and they wouldn't be as lucky as I am. I mean there are people who worked voluntary for nothing, so therefore the CE scheme was a few bob.

It depends what they want to do, and if their CE scheme is covering the skills that they need to do that, which they're not, of course. Very few CE schemes that I know involve computer training, which everybody's talking about computers. Certainly mine never was. Right, I could get one hundred pounds off my CE money and go out and train, but that was something I had to take on board. My understanding of CE schemes was that it was to develop skills for you to meet the economic boom that was out there. I don't think they are. I think a lot of employers abuse them also.

And because of the major failure of CE structures to create progression routes to the skilled labour market, they were in many ways treated as non-jobs:

I know a lot of CE schemes are worthwhile jobs and they're jobs that wouldn't be done otherwise, but people don't see them as real jobs, because they know they're only there for a limited time, you know, so you get people, they go in with good intentions, but after a while, if they get bored, it's like, "Well, I'm here for the money. Hopefully, I'll get a second year out of it."

The consequence has been that time limitations in the regulations have an even more adverse impact, with women caught between CE or returning to social welfare payments. Women have tried to get a renewal of their place, without success:

You know that other girl that was there on Friday, _____, her job is gone now, in December, she only got two year, she's finished in December. Your man said that they had to let so many, I think it's five, go. But we won't know till October, 'cos we're over thirty-five, myself and the other

> *three girls, so we won't know what's happening with us till*
> *then . . . So it was _____, _____, _____, and*
> *_____. Them four, they'll be finishing in December.*

And yet for some women they have been genuinely fulfilling. In two youth work projects up and running as a result of CE provision, the women involved were enthusiastic and committed. But the incapacity of the state system to translate these into ongoing jobs meant that, for one scheme, the value of the work and the relationships built up would all be lost, unless women could continue as unpaid volunteers and could solve the problem of childcare:

> *You'd get some say, "Well, I'm after losing the scheme, but*
> *I'll stick with them [as a volunteer]." But then, if you've*
> *young kids to be minded, you still have to pay a babysitter*
> *to mind them while you're doing your clubs.*

As part of her work for her diploma course, one woman wrote a project development plan for an after-school club for children which actually went on to be funded. The project has provided the children with teaching materials, including computers and overhead projectors. The project has been staffed using a CE scheme. In this instance, as a result of the woman's knowledge of poorly run CE schemes, she encouraged the training ideas of the project supervisor who took the issue of personal development of the CE workers very seriously:

> *She's never been a FÁS CE supervisor, so we both do the*
> *training together. But she's brilliant at supporting and*
> *everything. Like the first week of training with the girls,*
> *she delivered them sessions and it was personal develop-*
> *ment, and she was real like, "You're special, celebrate you."*
> *Like, she's built them up no end, I mean there's a couple on*
> *the workforce that have left school at thirteen and fourteen*
> *and have never worked, they've worked at cleaning jobs,*
> *but they've never actually gone into a real boss, signed a*
> *wages sheet, it would be like money into the hands, clean-*
> *ing stuff, you know. And they're coming on brilliant. They*
> *really are, it's great to see, they've really gelled well, as*
> *well.*

And, for all the problems attached to CE schemes, the distress caused by the announcement late in the summer of 1999 that CE schemes would be axed, was real:

> *Well, automatically in this _____, in December, three peo-*
> *ple will be struck from the CE scheme, because of Mary*
> *what's-her-name's [Harney] decision on schemes. So, three*
> *people will be losing out on jobs there now in December.*

Women have also found it difficult to pursue further education courses and diplomas, that lead on to skilled employment. Without sponsorship, it is extremely difficult for women to combine their studies with their family duties and with part-time paid work as well. One woman described dropping out for these reasons:

> *I started doing an NCVA Level Two. . . . And I was after*
> *doing a diploma. But it was in childcare, it was in Health,*
> *Hygiene and Safety. Now, I was on me way to distinctions*
> *in the lot of it. But they wouldn't apply for an extension for*
> *me . . . They told me there was an embargo and that I*
> *couldn't get an extension. . . . Then they wouldn't offer me*
> *the sponsorship either. . . . So I said, ah, I'll call it a day,*
> *you know. There was no way I could do an NCVA because*
> *I needed to go and look for work. I mean, with five kids,*
> *you know. So, I left it.*

The tragedy of this is that the potential of inner-city women to transform the educational environment is very great indeed. Much has been written about the need for an educational system that is more reflexive to the realities and needs of children and adults living in circumstances of social exclusion (see Lynch, 1998). To be able to equip women, who have their experience of child-rearing and a real commitment to working with children and young people, would pay back enormous dividends in the community. The exchange below, about working as teaching assistants in local schools, gives an indication of this potential:

> *We do teachers' assistants, two days a week over in the*
> *boys' school. And it's going well, now, go into the class*
> *with one of the teachers, say she has twenty or thirty in the*

class, just give some of them help with their work in English, Maths.

I think they [teachers] do need them [assistants] because there's an awful lot in the one class, now. There's a lot of pressure on the teacher. There's a lot of pressure on them trying to watch, say, five and trying to watch the other five and then there's ten.

Some of the kids is slower than the others, you know that way, they need more time to sit with.

We kind of help with that, like.

There's a new thing set up, there's one teacher, she's like a counselling teacher, but there's one teacher and myself, the teacher's assistant, and there's only two kids in the class. That's just for the time being, until they build up a relationship with them and get them to do their work, and then they'll be bringing in other kids, you know.

You see today, we go back now today at a quarter past one and we bring them down to the sports hall to play football or hockey or whatever.

If work like this was properly underwritten by the state and accompanied by good-quality, accredited training, it could translate into real ongoing work of greatest importance in helping to change how young people view education in the inner city, as Byrne (1998) has suggested (see footnote six in Chapter One above, page 12).

For the time being at least, there is an expansion of jobs in the construction industry and associated work for young people. Changes in the interface between the social welfare system and the labour market, like the Whole-Time Jobs Initiative, are making it easier for young men to participate in paid employment:

A lot of people are going into legit work now, because there's so many jobs now. Social Welfare are making it easier for people now. Before, it would be like, if you're in a job, you give up your book, which is impossible to do if you're raising a family.

However, women are ambivalent about the fact that their nearly adult children have been able to work in the expanding Docklands area. Immediate work and wage gains have encouraged young men to leave school as soon as possible:

> *The best part of them is working on that site. The best part of young lads is after coming out of school and didn't want to further their education, they're on it. And the local fellas, they put a lot of local fellas on it as well, that has kids.*

> *There's no shortage of work, like there's loads of work around there to be done. It's just that there's some of them selling drugs and they'd rather sell their drugs than work.*

> *My brother got an apprenticeship out of it.*

There is a feeling that work is keeping some young people away from heroin and that as a result, the locality is slightly calmer than it has been:

> *Because it's keeping them busy, it's keeping them off the streets. Because there's an awful lot of young lads working.*

> *It's keeping them occupied. But, even in the nights now, it's real quiet, do you know, like, people come in from work and they're having their dinner, or they're just tired, they just stay in, you don't see them really, as much standing around as they used to.*

> *But it's great to even see them running to work every morning, and they come home with their lunch, with their hats on.*

> *It gives them that more confidence, as well, that they're bringing in a week's wages and they're probably appreciated. 'Cos they're working for it, you know what I mean? And they have the work to go to.*

The concern is that when the jobs disappear, when the building boom ends, there will have been no training to enable these young men to transfer to different skilled sectors of the economy:

This is it, they're back on the streets again when the jobs are gone.

They have nothing, and then they're back to square one, aren't they? Back in their rooms, sitting in their rooms, thinking about drugs, because that's all they can think of isn't it, they've nothing else to think.

There's some of the companies now, like, that they'd have more work on and they'll probably keep them on, shift them to somewhere else.

Like, usually some building sites go for three years, some go for five years, so if they find that they're good workers, they'll sort of bring them with them, you know, if they get stuck in.

Nevertheless, this new influx of jobs runs counter to much of what the black economy has been: one of low-paid, off-the-books work, or no legitimate work at all, combined with the illegal economics of large-scale theft that has accompanied heroin:

That's another culture in the area that's acceptable. They look at it, well they're only robbing shops, they're not robbing people's houses, and they're not robbing handbags. They're only earning a living and I'm getting it cheap. It suits everyone. I've often bought meself, and I'm being honest. I've often rang friends and said, "They're selling this perfume, do you want some?" Tell them the price, "Ah, yeah, get us two bottles", you know. And it does go on everywhere, it goes on more so in the inner city because it's acceptable. It's just seen as a fact of life, you know. And with people in poverty, if they are only on the book, it is an easy way to get what they want for their kids.

BUILDING SUPPORT FOR CHILDREN: SUMMER PROJECTS AND OTHER YOUTH ACTIVITIES

Just as with the awareness that work availability for young people plays a role in modifying the attractiveness of heroin, there is a strong sense from women that prevention work for younger children and teenagers must include excellent local youth facilities. And up to the present there has been far too little:

> There's absolutely nothing there at the moment. They're doing well, considering. I mean, we've lost one generation completely, you know what I mean, I'm talking about the fifteen to eighteen, nineteen-year-olds, they're lost in general.

> There's nowhere for the kids to play at the moment. Like, there's a park being built around there, and it's being built the last two years and it's still not finished. And for the size of the park that's to cater for this community, it's unreal.

> It won't be big enough.

> I'd like to see more money coming in for the youth, to build up something for them, that'll keep them going for a couple of year. And keep them off the streets.

> There's nothing in the area, as such. They're trying to get the clubs, they still have the clubs going, but it's not the same as years ago, you know, when the leaders would say, "You do this and you're barred." And you'd be afraid you'd be barred, and you wouldn't do it. But now the kids are like, "So, bar me." They've a major attitude now, and yet you always try to keep them occupied.

These observations relate to two of the three distinct micro-communities within the north inner city where the fieldwork for this project was located. In the third, there was a sense that the basic resources have been put in place in the last several years, but that there is insufficient leadership and youth work to connect with young people and make those resources an option that young people would want to take up:

> They have a lot of facilities and amenities around them, but they have the problem down there as well that they have to go knocking on kids' doors, to bring the kids to these things, you know.

It may be easier to engage with much younger children and it could be argued that a long-term prevention strategy should start

with the very young age groups and work on building those relationships over a long period of years. Summer projects for children can be such a starting point and, in one community, a handful of women have worked hard to establish one with depth and
scope enough to make it attractive to children up to the age of 13.
However, it was only in 1999 that they were given local authority
funding and back-up, and there was some doubt that this would
continue to be extended to them:

> *It started with a residents' association meeting, and every-*
> *one was giving out, "There's nothing for the kids, there's*
> *nothing for the kids." So, we decided to run a summer pro-*
> *ject. That was five years ago. Four years ago.*

For the first three years, the project ran on a very part-time basis,
with a trip one day a week over a period of six weeks. In 1999, with
grants from Dublin Corporation and two of the youth organisations, the women were able to create a more substantial project
over a period of four weeks:

> *It's got bigger, this year was really big. It started off with a*
> *trip a week for maybe six weeks, and a party at the end of*
> *it. And this year, we decided to do something different and it*
> *was very hard. We had four weeks, intense weeks. . . . To get*
> *the insurance and the grants, we had to have it over the*
> *four weeks, or you could have had it shorter. But we decided*
> *to go for the four.*

The grant from the Corporation helped to pay for the insurance,
while the other smaller grants and donations from local businesses enabled them to keep the costs down. The most expensive
away trip was five pounds and such activities as pitch and putt
were donated or financed locally:

> *We had Arts and Crafts for the under-tens once a week, we*
> *had pitch-and-putt for the over-tens once a week. We had,*
> *it was supposed to be snooker, but it didn't work out so we*
> *had bowling for the over-tens once a week, and disco-*
> *dancing for the over-tens once a week. We had swimming*
> *for everybody once a week and we had a trip every week,*
> *and we had two different drama things.*

Running a total of three days a week for three weeks and five days a week for the final week, the project provided in all 700 day spaces of supervised play over the entire period, with 50 children participating each week. However, the project suffered from a lack of support from parents in the local community:

> *Which turned out very, very well. But we'd no support. Believe it or not, we'd no support.*

> *An odd time, you'd get a parent coming.*

> *We begged for help, when we put the leaflets out.*

> *We actually sat in the _____ for registration, like four eejits, meself and _____ was down one morning from ten till eleven.*

> *We decided to do a morning, an afternoon and an evening so that everyone had a chance to do it, and we were just sitting there, basically, and then people knocking at your door three days later wanting to join. We were sitting in the _____, they didn't have to walk anywhere.*

> *They'd knock up to your door then a few days later and say, "Oh, I forgot about it", or "I was wondering what you were sitting there for." You know, as if you would sit on the step, you could have been doing better than sitting on the step, with bits of paper in your hand. And the idea was for them to pay a week in advance. It worked, kind of, the first week, but then you were getting it [money] in dribs and drabs, and you don't know who's given you what.*

This indicates the need for long-term community development work in the area to build that process of support. The lack of it put pressure on the women who did at least have some part-time input from a Dublin Corporation youth worker:

> *We would have been lost without her.*

> *It was tough going, because meself and _____, _____ works in the morning and I worked in the evening. I was running to do me own house, running back down to go to the _____, to give a hand there, running*

back then, trying to sort out me own place and then having to work, go to the disco-dancing, and going from the disco-dancing then, to work.

And then we'd trips with the over-tens, there was someone going with the over-tens, and just say they went, you were minding their younger child, with yours, because yours weren't old enough to go. You were juggling all the time. Which meant you couldn't do anything even if you wanted to.

You'd need parental support. I understand people have different stuff, but there's some people that are just sitting there, doing nothing, you know, and just can't be bothered.

They just send the kids out, you know and we'll look after them, and that's not the point, the point is we all pull together, you know. They're sitting there for the day, and we're looking after their kids. Like, we weren't asked to do it, we took it on, like I enjoy doing it, but when you think you're running from one thing to the other, and your own kids are left because you're giving so much time to others. It's all right if people can't make it, you know what I mean, I can understand that, but when you know that some of them are just sitting there, you know what I mean, it's very hard. So you don't get enough support.

Yeah, because it actually got to the stage that it cost me more, because I had to take time off work. I had to get someone to cover for me, so I could go on some of the trips.

The only support we had was from one person in the flats that has no children. She was giving us money, and she has done it every year. She had kids but they're grown up. She has no reason to give anything.

Say if only one of us had to go on one day, if we had someone from the Corporation, just say. If there was more help, you'd have the courage. But there was no way, I think we were all nearly heading for a breakdown.

The women budgeted carefully and even though it would have been permissible to pay wages for a part-time co-ordinator with one of the grants they obtained (which could have been one of them), they chose instead to put it into the kitty so that the schedule of activities would be as varied as possible for the children. Thus, they turned down the possibility of being paid for their input. At the end of the summer period, they did have concerns about their own families:

> *Well, they benefit in the activities and the trips, but they don't benefit 'cos they're not getting enough time, they lose out on the attention they'd normally get from their mother.*

On the other hand, they were convinced of the value of the project for the children in general:

> *I have to say that even though some of them was going around saying, "This is stupid, this it thick, this is crap," but they were the very ones that was turning up first.*

> *The kids are more united, they get on better during the summer project. Like, you'd look over . . . and you'd see the kids and there'd be killing, you know, there could be two kids in particular there, killing each other, and you'd go off for the day trip with them and they're great. . . . There's a few kids . . . who are really, really wild kids . . . Bring them off for the day and they're different kids. These are small kids, like six, seven-year-olds, and they run wild . . . and when you bring them off for the day, they were great.*

> *Take them away and they're different. You know, some kids are never brought out. . . . There is children who are never brought as far as _____, and that's the truth, you know. And it was something for them to look forward to. And also you had a hold over them: "Well, you do it again, and you're not coming on the next trip." If they did get out of line.*

So summer projects, if they were sufficiently resourced and developed within the community could have an ongoing impact for younger children. Sports and athletics offer another option for older children and in the three localities, there were efforts being made to revive clubs and sporting activities which had fallen away in recent years. Football has been popular in the past, but in two localities, heroin addiction had wiped out some early promise:

> *When we were applying for funding . . . we sent them in with the application, with the proposal, a photograph of a football team. And at the time, they were all ten or eleven, and they'd be all the sixteen, seventeen age group now. And every single one of them is either locked up, on drugs or dead.*

> *There used to be a load of young fellas down here that was great footballers, and they could have got somewhere, and then just turned straight to the drugs. You know, like, they had people there to train them and keep them occupied, and something else just happened and they just got onto it, you know.*

This indicates above all else how intensely consuming the relationship with heroin can become. Nonetheless, football is still seen as an important alternative activity for young people. One group of women currently involved in youth work described how a local game could still draw 40 or 50 onlookers:

> *You always know where to find your child, around on the pitch.*

> *Well, this evening they will be, it'll be packed now, about six o'clock this evening.*

They were attempting to get financial support to build a proper pitch locally. There are also attempts to revive athletics and, following just after the period of the drugs marches, the north inner city had an athletics team entered for the first time in the national Community Games:

> *The kids did very well, some of them got through to the finals, and that's as far as they went. But they did very well, considering they'd only six weeks practice. And that club is still going to this day . . . But they are Leinster champions and all this, they've gold medals, you'd want to see them, they're brilliant. And the Community Games is not good enough for them now, they're into bigger and better things now, you know.*

Local Gardaí have begun to help out with this athletics club. Drama work is also providing a focus for children and younger teenagers and women continue to work with the more traditional notion of clubs where children come and pay an entrance fee to help pay for games and equipment:

> *We run two clubs, Monday and Thursday, from eight to ten, aged from eight. So we have no funding for them, now, they pay fifty pence in and we kind of do something with that, you know. And then the youth club is on Tuesday night, Wednesday night girls' club, and they're from eleven to sixteen.*

One of the localities has been very badly off with no premises even to begin a community centre. A local group marched on the current Taoiseach's constituency office and finally won a promise for new facilities in the area which hold out the hope for new directions and potential in the community:

> *Something positive is happening. So, there's a building advisory group that's going to be looking after that, looking at the plans and making suggestions. As it is, they've gone around, looking at different communities, to look at their centres, to get ideas, that kind of thing.*

Women are not so naïve, however, as to conclude that facilities alone will help to rebuild their areas unless there is a commitment to long-term sustainability of both process and community development on the part of the local authority, local partnerships and the state:

> *So, I'm not under any illusion that a sports centre or a community centre is going to solve all the problems. And they're in the process of employing another youth development officer and a youth worker. I don't know, if I was in their shoes I wouldn't know where to start.*

But there are beginnings which could build on past experiences. Insufficient funding has been a huge problem, however, for the local and voluntary efforts currently in place:

The big problem is the funding, really, you need money for them, to keep it interesting, to keep the club interesting, and to keep the kids, you know.

That was like us, we used to have three drama groups run-ning for the kids, and then, like that the funding, we used to get funded from _____, and that all stopped because they weren't doing the certain funding that we were looking for. Like, there's only certain fundings that they're doing, and they'll send us out an application, but if you're hopeful, you'll get it, if not you're not.

Interviewer: Is there nowhere else that you could go for it?

Like, a few sponsors and that, like, from people. And then we got a thousand pounds from the Arts Council about three months ago, but we haven't seen it yet. We went to local businesses and asked them for sponsors.

There's not enough money put into the clubs for the kids down here, and they haven't got the insurance or the money to bring them on weekend trips, or even full-day trips, only allowed to, say, _____ and the _____. That's as far as they can stretch to, you know that way, like, if there was more money put into the clubs for the kids, I'd say you'd get a lot more kids, and the clubs would run even better.

None of the women interviewed on the subject of youth work, clubs, football and so on appeared to know about the setting up by the government in 1998 of the Young Persons Facilities and Services Fund to help fund sport and recreation in localities where heroin use is a major issue. This has resulted, however, in a plan being de-veloped for the north inner city which was spearheaded by the North Inner City Drugs Task Force and submitted to the national fund. With approval for 27 projects, this should begin to make a dif-ference to the work that women have pinpointed here as vital.

DRUGS EDUCATION PROJECTS

Drugs education projects in the inner city have often arisen from the needs of parents who have suffered the loss of children to her-oin and parents who are anxious to understand more about the physical, psychological and emotional consequences of drug use. There is much to learn and much to make sense of, because of the way the drugs scene itself has changed and continues to evolve. Ecstasy has created a distinct sub-culture of use, for example:

> *People on speed and people on heroin, they're different cultures, you speak different lingo. But people on E, anyone that's ever done an E, even now, could relate to someone that's doing an E now. I could relate to a teenager that's doing E. And you know, you've only to say a certain word, and the conversation will fly along. 'Cos it is a culture, the E is another culture as well.*

Newer patterns of use like this raise issues, however, of the gaps in understanding between what pharmacology knows of the actions of drugs and what beliefs and practices actually are. At an Eastern Health Board-funded meeting of family support groups in November 1998, one of the women spoke about a talk they had been given on drugs by a scientist, who assured them that the pharmacological action of heroin would not help to cope with the extreme "highs" that ecstasy produces. And yet this is an established pattern for a minority of young people now involved in regular ecstasy use (Murphy-Lawless et al., 2000). These beliefs amongst young people create changes in practices and patterns of use which parents need to know if they are to offer relevant and informed support to their children. To offer poor or inaccurate information erases the value of drugs education for young people (ibid.; Coveney et al., 1999).

Volunteer drugs education projects which have emerged in the north inner city have been assisted and supported in their formation by the voluntary sector which has been working for a very long time to create a more responsive public policy to the heroin issue. As stated earlier, the Inter-Agency Drugs Project was established by ICON in the early 1990s and became the North Inner City Drugs Task Force in 1997, once the government moved to set up a structure of local drugs task forces. As part of its work, the NICDTF established an education and prevention sub-group. Moving on from that time, a coalition of voluntary groups in the City-Wide Campaign against Drugs held meetings throughout the greater Dublin area, urging the formation of education sub-groups.

Through groups like these, interested women in the north inner city gained a familiarity and understanding of how young people were actually engaging in drug use. It was from this background that one woman became involved with more formal coursework on drugs education:

> _____ *from the* _____ *rang me and said there was a course happening and would I be interested in going on it. And I decided at the time that I wanted to go on and learn more about drugs and all that kind of stuff, and eventually work in it in some shape or form. I didn't know what way that was. Because I was saying about feeling inadequate, I said "Well maybe if I know a bit more, I might be able to help if these people come along." I hadn't a clue what I was letting meself in for . . . So, when I went out I knew some of the faces from different meetings, I would have known some of them over years . . . As it turned out, they're a great group. Obviously, it started with fifteen or sixteen and went down to about eight, but that can be only expected, you know. It's good crack, and sometimes it doesn't go the way I want it to go, you know. I found, the first year was training, the whole first year, nearly, was training, yeah. And part of the training they got _____ in to provide basic or foundation facilitation skills training. I found it tough, because I'd regard myself as being shy, believe it or not, and standing up in front of people and talking, I'd run a mile from that, but it has built up the confidence.*

Another woman had come through an addiction to ecstasy herself but due not to that so much as a family member's tragic involvement with heroin, she decided she wanted to take a proactive stance in education:

> *Well, I was always interested in drugs because of my own addiction . . . I was interested to see how a community functioned round drugs. And when I found out what it actually was, which was about giving back information to the community, educating the community, that was the main reason why I got involved in it, and educating myself at the one time, you know. That's mainly why I got involved. The way I justified it was I don't mind any other*

*drug, but I'm against heroin. Heroin was what killed
_____, so I'm against heroin. Now, if it had been ecstasy
that killed _____, I probably wouldn't have went
against it, because I know they're great. And I knew that,
and I've been there. There was many times I was offered
heroin and I'd say no. And they'd be saying, "Just take a
smoke, you'll get a brilliant sleep and you'll wake up real
fresh." And I'm like, "No, you're all right, I don't want it."
Because I knew what hash was like and hash did not agree
with me at all, I didn't like it, it made me paranoid, it made
me stupid, I lost control of me body. Whereas with E and
speed and all, you're still in control, you're more alert. So
that's why I didn't like the downers.*

The process of training and becoming accustomed to addressing
meetings was integral to enabling women volunteers to knit together in a comprehensive picture what street information they had
about drug-use patterns, young people's needs, current blockages in
the way the treatment system runs and the needs of parents. An
important aspect of having this resource in the community was that
parents and adults could know more about available options for
younger drug users:

*I did, what I did was a certificate in counselling skills. But
it covered all aspects of community work, and it gave me a
whole different perspective on the thing. Plus the fact that
there were forty people in the course, all from different
walks of life, and listening to their anger and their frustration. People who lost children through drugs, I mean that
was a huge impact on me, too.*

*The best training I ever did was the diploma first, and then
going on to the _____. Definitely . . . I met up with mothers and fathers who were experiencing their children going through the drug scene, and that's where I seen from a
totally different aspect of it. And I'm seeing these mothers
and they're absolutely heartbroken. Because, at the check-
in, although they wouldn't go into too much detail, you'd
know, like, their son is acting up, their daughter is acting
up, they're at their wits' end. And it was horrible to see.
And it really opened your eyes . . . I'm like, if my child goes
on drugs, I'm going to end up like these, I'm going to be*

desperate. By that time, please God they won't go on drugs, but by that time I want straight away answers, I don't want them on a waiting list for three months, or I don't want her on a waiting list for a year. I want help for them, there and then . . . You know, prevention and education first of all, then educating the parents, and then eventually work for solutions. You know, immediate solutions, not these waiting lists, there's too many of them. I mean, there's children fifteen and sixteen that won't go to their parents, but they won't go for treatment because they need their parents' consent. Which means they're getting heavier and heavier into the drug scene. I mean, if there was a way around that, that their parents didn't need to know. I know there is no way at the minute, but if there was a way around it, I think you'd find an awful lot more kids looking for help, rather than waiting till they're eighteen.

After training work, members of this drugs education group moved on to give drugs education training in a variety of settings in the north inner city:

I did the _____, and I thought it was a wonderful experience meeting these women, and they certainly had a lot to contribute to it.

When a group approaches us and asks can somebody come and give a session on, be it HIV, AIDS, whatever, I've found that I was the one to put meself forward. Or because nobody else was putting their name forward, I'd go, "Well, I'll do it", you know. And at the time I was working and I was doing the night shift, I was finding it very hard. But now that I'm not there, it's grand, that's what I want to do. I've decided that, like, we hope sometime in the future to get funded to employ somebody, preferably one of us, to do administration, or co-ordinate the group. Go out and promote the group, that would be the kind of thing, because we could get a lot of work at this stage. You know, we're getting there, we're getting there slowly, so it's all positive stuff.

I've decided that I'm going to put as much time as possible into that.

Well, firstly, for me personally, I got an insight into people and their communities. Even though they're from the same community, each have difference experiences in their lives. So that gave me an insight. It was an opportunity also. I would never have gotten the facilitation course; it was an opportunity to education. . . . The most positive was the opportunity to get a look at the bigger picture.

But, when we go into a group, we always tell them that we don't know everything. And if something comes up that we don't have the answer to there and then, we take the question and we get the answers and get back to them on it. So, the group were delighted with the sessions we gave . . . So, what we do after each session with a group, all the materials we've used we put in to a pile and we keep a note of how the session went, how we did, and it's just like a reference, if anyone else ever wants to do a group like that.

At time of interview, this group was working towards the creation of a full-time post but like other groups in the north inner city, it lacked sufficient institutional resources to draw on for prevention and education work:

I found there was an anger in me because I thought the government was putting it back on us to do something about this. Here we were, volunteers, taking time out. Because this was all voluntary work. And I thought in many ways they could have put a value on our work, and gave us some sort of, if not accreditation, then some sort of financial support. I mean, we were getting funding, but nothing, just what we needed.

And the funding, we were only funded for a year. So after the year we decided that we were all getting on so well and we were enjoying the group so much, that we would keep it up. 'Cos we didn't need an awful lot of money to keep the group going, and the whole idea was that we would go out and pass on what we had learned, possibly with the chance of being paid as well, at some stage, or in some cases, you know. So, that's what's happening at the moment.

In meeting with a range of people and groups in the community, members of this group have come to identify different perspectives around treatment. For example, methadone maintenance is seen by many as problematic:

I knew a lot about drugs but it was only through listening to the women in that, that I really got a ground level insight into what was going on in these people's lives. Their fears around methadone, stabilisation, their fears around drugs, the way they were looking towards all the time and they weren't settling for, there was no middle of the road for them, everything was black and white, it was either drugs or drug-free. I think a lot of them still think like that. But what I'm seeing now is those who want drug-free, and I'm saying harm reduction, but I think we complement each other. Because neither of our ways is right or wrong. We're all struggling there, and we're doing something.

Give them the methadone and you keep them happy . . . I think that's the whole problem between the EHB, the government and everyone else, give them the money, give the clinics, open up plenty of clinics, plenty of methadone and keep them there . . . Keep them at the same level.

I don't know if we're doing the right thing around methadone. I think it has a purpose in terms of long-term drug-users who, because of the effects of drugs on the brain, will need methadone, it is a medication. I think it's not the answer. I think we should concentrate more on education, if it's only to prolong the start of drug use. And that takes a lot of effort. It means introducing people to a new way of life, changing people's attitudes. So, it's going to be long, hard.

There's gaps in the services that's provided. There's no, in the communities that I was in, a drop-in centre, where people counsel and are available for people. I know they need support groups, and again the women have set up support groups and they are excellent. Addiction doesn't stop. Opening centres from ten o'clock in the morning till half five is not, you know what I mean? What do these people do? If we're going to teach people a way of life, we need to provide a service for them in terms of how to ex-

*perience life without drugs. There's huge gaps, of course
there's huge gaps.*

Because of the way the drugs scene changes for young people,
there is an urgent need to get good up-to-date information and
education programmes going in the schools:

*I would like to see them in the schools, in the curriculum in
the schools, part of it. People are all the time talking about
drugs, and educating people to drugs. I am saying, educate people to their needs, and to identify their needs, because all drug use is need-satisfying. So we've got to firstly
recognise that people do have needs, and how they meet
those needs in an effective way. But we've got to address
that they have needs. I think there's a lot of emphasis in
schools on drugs, and I think people are rebelling, some
people are saying we're actually educating them to drugs,
to use drugs, and in many ways, I can understand that,
where it would be better to educate them to meet their
needs in more effective ways.*

*The changes have been that they're getting younger, the
drug users, that we're at the moment going through a
phase where it's coke, rather than heroin, and we certainly
have to get a handle on the benzos, because they're definitely out of control. That's the changes I see.*

PROCESS AND PARTICIPATION

Throughout all the interviews and sessions, women were keenly
observant about the processes they had seen the wider community
undergoing. Specifically, in relation to heroin, there was a strong
feeling that the community would have to continue to live with it,
even though many women might hope for a drug-free option.
Asked whether they saw an end to heroin use and heroin dealing,
women spoke about the future this way:

*No, that'll never end, that'll keep going on and on and on,
the drugs. I mean, one will stop and then someone else will
take over, that's what happens down here. One stops dealing and someone else takes over, they stop dealing and
someone else takes over. It'll never end, sure it's going on*

years and years. You'll never stop drugs, there's too much money to be made in it as well, do you know what I mean?

They're getting younger, the kids that's doing it now, and there's nothing around here for them at all, nothing. They're laughing at it going on and they're watching them doing it and all. I hate to see what's going on now, around my kids as well.

Two issues arise immediately in relation to this perceived reality. First of all, what needs to be said or done for younger mothers who are facing into an uncertain future with their children? Secondly, is there any way to make available a comprehensive and positive *long-term* prevention strategy to build different futures for children and young people? Women were discouraged on both counts, as the following dialogue illustrates. Although they see the importance of building mutual support within the community, this sounds at times almost a strategy of desperation in how it is put forward. They have seen too little help and support coming to themselves as mothers and therefore to younger mothers from any official quarter:

Yeah, to get together and help one another.

It doesn't seem like the drug problem is going to go away, seems like it's just getting worse.

Because I mean there's no-one out there that's going to help, so I think the only thing is to get together and help one another and fight, fight for their rights, fight for what they need, not for what they want, fight for what they need. I mean they will need other support besides, we need other support besides us just meeting.

There was concern that in not developing sufficient and widely available long-term aftercare and support programmes for users, along with prevention work, the gains that have been made would be stripped away:

They don't give anything away, the government doesn't.

They want to put it into aftercare. And put more money into prevention, aftercare and recovery, I mean preven-

> *tion is for the ones that's going to go on it, aftercare and recovery is for the kids that's on it, that's going to be on it for the rest of their life, because I can't see them stopping. It's too hard.*

> *It's probably back on the streets as well because the marches stopped . . . There's about thirty on these steps to-night, that hasn't been for a long, long time, but they're back.*[3]

New street retailing patterns emerge rapidly with illegal drugs, with new combinations of methadone, amphetamines, prescription drugs, ecstasy, cocaine and of course, heroin being used by young people. Thus, at a purely practical level, there is a need to disseminate accurate and ongoing information:

> *We really need people coming in, I mean we, like, we have children on drugs, right, but we don't know everything, as much as we think we do. We would still need to be educated, because there's all these new drugs coming out.*

This requirement, however, raises an issue which emerged at so many points, namely of ongoing, secure funding to support work in the community around prevention and education. There was a feeling of intense frustration around this and a feeling of women's work not counting or being recognised:

> *I mean if you need people to come in to talk to you, you need funding to pay these people, 'cos they're not going to do it for nothing. So who do we apply for funding? Do you know what I mean? Can't apply to the government 'cos they don't know we exist.*

> *The task force will fund you maybe for a year and if you keep going after that like, you don't get any funding.*

At the same time, women have set themselves clear agendas and know how they wish to advance the work in which they have been involved, as with this woman:

---

[3] This comment was made in June 1999, when anti-drugs activities had re-emerged.

To be able to go out and speak to other groups, and start up other support groups, because there's an awful lot of women out there, an awful lot of mothers out there crying out for help that doesn't know where to go, doesn't know what to do about it, like us in the beginning, and to find the different places to go to, and try and set up somewhere for them, and set up the support groups, and be able to go out and be able to talk to them.

There was concern about how difficult it has been on the one hand to engage with bodies like Dublin Docklands Authority on re-development in the north inner city and on the other hand to maintain community-wide involvement in proposed housing and re-development plans. One group had recently approached the Docklands Authority for a contribution to their football programme and been given only £250 (€317.43):

We went down to them like that as well, and they gave us £250 sponsor, that was for a mention in the programme as well.

As far as the community was concerned, in a locality which has had no play facilities at all in the recent past, this was a serious breach of trust about which they could not exercise any effective protest. The women argued that play spaces were to have been constructed before new private apartments buildings were constructed:

It is unbelievable that they're putting up all these apartments and houses and buildings, and they won't give the kids somewhere to play.

The playground was supposed to be built first, before the apartments.

Like, they're shooting up over the top of the houses now, and that park still isn't finished. That was promised before them apartments.

They don't care, once they're making that money, they're not interested and you're just part of the community, that's it. They're not going to be worried about us and what we think, once them buildings is going up and they're getting a hundred and odd grand for one apartment. And look at the apartments that they're after building. Now, there's money. You're talking about millions, millions you're talking about. I mean, it's £110,000 for one apartment, think about it. And I wouldn't even mind, but they're not even finished and they're bought, most of them is bought. Already, most of them is bought, sold, and they're not even finished yet.

And yet the community itself is not secure about building and sustaining a process of participation, not least because of the damaging relations associated with the anti-drugs marches:

They found it hard to get people interested again, because if you were on any committee, you were seen to be a vigilante. So, they found it hard to get people on board. So, when the redevelopment plan for the flats came in, people showed an interest, and they had an open day, they had a model as well, where you put the whole lot up, and when they had the crowd in, they took advantage of it, and asked would people come forward and go on the committee. A fair number put their names forward, but they realised when they looked at it, that the people who put their names forward were either people that were in the blocks that were getting knocked down, who wanted to be in there, and they wanted to know what houses they were getting, they'd get first-hand information on the committee.

I don't blame the committee, I blame the people down here, 'cos they will not get out and they won't fight for their rights.

It's the same people all the time.

There were doubts about the decisions and non-decisions the community had taken in dealing with redevelopment in the area:

We should have just got them flats refurbished . . . See, that's what happens down here, the minute they see a bit of land, that's it, they're in for the kill, "'Ah, we'll build something here." Did you see that bank that was built down there as well, the Bank of Ireland? I believe inside it, it's something else. There's a few of the local women, now, working in there cleaning, you know, six to eight in the evening, and said that it's massive inside, massive. They have the money.

It's crazy, once you have that bit of power, they can do what they like. To us, we're just ordinary Joe Soap people, they're not going to worry about the likes of us down here, or say, _____ or _____, they're going to do their own thing and they're making money out of it. They're not going to be bothered about us.

Some parts of the planning process which were deeply objectionable have been halted, however:

There was a bit of a meeting over the high-rise buildings, the back of _____, now they brought the plans into the _____. That was the time where she'd have got all the women together. She brought in the plans, she said, "That's exactly what they're going to try to do to you." Say this is _____, and this is my house, you'd have been in darkness. So they didn't go ahead with that in any case.

There was a thing put in against them high-rise buildings. Because people aren't going to be paying rent to be living in darkness . . . Bigger than Liberty Hall, one of them was. So people said, no, they weren't having it.

Some women did feel more encouraged about their own housing being redeveloped:

The people will be rehoused who are living in them, they have to be rehoused. But as people are moving out now, they're not putting anyone else into them. They're boarding them up. It'll look horrible for a while, but the plan is to move out a whole block, because people are giving out, they don't want to go, but they're planning to move out, say, this block, and they're giving them temporary accommodation in another flat, and they're getting in and refurbishing the whole block, and then letting them move back in. They have had work. The most recent job we've had is the central heating installed, which is a godsend, it's brilliant. Gas.

One woman reflected a strongly felt perspective that the futures of both inner city communities and of women living there would not be avoided for much longer by the government:

> *Firstly, the women are open to more education, and I think women are being heard now. I thought it was very interesting, one time we did the voting thing with _____, and I thought that was very interesting, the fact that a lot of people are not educated to vote, and how important their vote is, that it can make a difference.*[4] *But I wouldn't in any way undermine the fact that the government still is made up of men and they will make the decision at the end of the day. I still think that what the government put into communities, certainly like the north inner city, marginalised, poor areas, it's a pittance.*
>
> *The government will need to take responsibility. They've thrown it all onto communities and they've thrown so much funding in, but really they're still hopping a lot. There need to be recreational centres provided . . . Nobody gives a damn what happens after that. So I really think the government needs to listen to the needs of the people.*

The experiences of these women point to the continuing need to build on processes in two areas: the first is to expand tangible education options and certification for women; the second is the work of supporting and sustaining local participation. The participants in this study are women who have emerged into the community as active participants. They have worked to obtain new levels of awareness, training and self-development. They are clear about the importance of the demands they have begun to articulate about education for themselves, and a better future for their families, and how these must be responded to comprehensively by the state. At the same time there are many more women who have yet to take the first step into wider community participation and learning. In trying to connect with this latter group of women, there are lessons to be learned from the women who have already moved into this new sphere. In this respect, the new Education Equality Initiative,

---

[4] The woman is referring to a session that her group did on voting and democratic processes.

depending on how it is introduced and integrated at local level, represents a real opportunity to engage with women and to develop a relevant participatory model of education.

The same also applies to the process of building relevant community participation strategies. With the downloading of new funding for capital projects in the north inner city community as urban renewal programmes finally gather pace, grounded strategies of participation at local level are crucial for the future well-being of the community.

Summary of Chapter Six

♦ *This chapter presents findings from women on their involvement with community-based groups relating to the following activities:*

  o *Self-development*

  o *Family support*

  o *Education and training*

  o *Children's play facilities and youth activities*

  o *Drugs education projects.*

♦ *Women have come to work at various levels in one or several of these areas as they have sought to take control of their lives and the life of their community.*

♦ *This work has frequently begun at the personal development level, where women are exploring ways to overcome the gendered impact of social exclusion. This is especially important for solving the problem of long-term poverty which women experience as a result of their status in households where they are dependent on social welfare or single parent allowances or on low-waged unskilled labour.*

♦ *There are special support needs for women who have children who are heroin users and family support groups have been a community response to those needs.*

♦ *Building a group structure which can guarantee confidentiality and then developing strategies such as stress management and other course work, counselling, and social events have enabled women to reclaim their lives and to balance their requirements against those of their family, especially the very difficult needs and demands of the child who is a heroin user or who is in treatment. The exchange of information and experience has also led to an often critical stance on the way official drugs treatment policies are evolving. The women made a strong argument for consistent long-term funding of this kind of group work, as an essential element of support for families directly affected by the constant crises that accompany heroin use and treatment.*

♦ *Women's groups are an excellent way to overcome a sense of isolation in north inner city communities. Community Employment (CE) schemes have been useful for helping women to break through a sense of depression and non-accomplishment.*

♦ *The challenge of something new has led women to take pre-training courses, including literacy, maths, and parenting skills, before going on to more formal training. Second-chance education has been a vital element for women who were early school-leavers. There is a range of settings provided by women's, community and unemployed centres in the north inner city, where women can access courses, some of which have led on to certificates and diplomas. Women feel that this has also enabled them to set a positive example for their children to follow, and this is linked to their aspiration for education and a better way of life for themselves and their children.*

♦ *They want further training and accreditation structures which relate to the needs of people who have endured social exclusion.*

♦ *However, women criticised the lack of progression routes from training courses and the failure to convert CE schemes into real jobs. For those women unable to participate in CE training, there are few or no alternative funded routes to achieve anything more for themselves.*

♦ *For women eligible for CE schemes, the work they have done for themselves and for their communities has been very useful, but there are hard questions asked about the quality of training in some cases and about government support to make these in to sustainable jobs. The availability of good quality work for them and their older children is seen as having a huge role to play in creating a challenge to the heroin sub-culture.*

♦ *Prevention work is seen in its widest sense by women as being the provision of play, sport and other activities for children and young people. Many of the localities in the north inner city have had no provision within recent years for such activities. Women have tried to make up this deficit, running summer projects, weekly clubs and sports clubs and neighbourhood football. Women expressed dismay at the problems of attracting ongoing long-term funding for these activities from the local authority, from the state agencies and from local businesses. They argued that the local areas need a long-term commitment in funds and staff to help rebuild their community.*

♦ *Community-run drugs education projects have been a special intervention to enable parents to learn more about the physical, psychological and social effects of drugs and the drugs culture. Their work has enabled them to develop different perspectives on treatment and prevention needs. But again, although women have trained formally for this work, including building up their facilitation skills, and have presented talks in many different settings, there is concern about the lack of long-term state funding for this important resource at local level.*

♦ *The final section of the chapter presents findings on the problems of process and participation which women have encountered as they have sought to prioritise community needs. Despite the effort women have made to take control of their lives and the lives of their communities, they identify a number of issues where they are deeply concerned about the problem of non-response.*

♦ *These include:*

  ○ *The need for mutual support strategies for younger mothers*

  ○ *The lack of long-term support and employment for drug users*

  ○ *The lack of long-term prevention and education work in the widest possible sense*

  ○ *The difficulty in meeting community needs through the state and private enterprise support as huge areas of the north inner city are re-capitalised.*

♦ *In these women's experience, the process of decision-making on these larger issues has not been inclusive. Their experiences stand as a salutary warning at a point when the initiatives on regeneration in the north-east inner city are taking shape. The experiences of these women point to the continuing need to build on processes in two areas: the first is to expand tangible education options and certification for women; the second is the work of supporting and sustaining local participation. The participants in this study have worked to obtain new levels of awareness, training and self-development and are clear about the importance of the demands they have begun to articulate about education. But there are many more women who have yet to take the first step into wider community participation and learning. In trying to connect with this latter group of women, there are lessons to be learned from the women who have already moved into this new sphere. In this respect, the new Education Equality Initiative represents a real opportunity to engage with women and to develop a relevant participatory model of education. That same requirement to be alert to the lessons and experiences coming out of the last five years applies just as strongly to the process of building relevant community participation strategies. As urban renewal programmes finally gather pace, grounded strategies of participation at local level are crucial for the future well-being of the community.*

Chapter Seven

RECOVERING ACTIVE CITIZENSHIP AND PARTICIPATION

TAKING SOCIAL EXCLUSION SERIOUSLY

The north inner city community bears the marks of the same critical pressures of rapid de-industrialisation, deepening unemployment, disadvantage, and urban decay which have converged on many major cities in Europe and the United States in the last decades of the twentieth century. Here, the community has also been at the epicentre of the heroin crisis, with the largest concentration of heroin users in the Irish state. The combined impact of these events has inflicted terrible damage on individuals, on families and on the social cohesion in the local community. In turn, this has had implications for social cohesion in the larger community and has laid down a challenge for the state. For some critics, this incapacity on the part of the state has amounted to a potential crisis of legitimation (Curtin and Varley, 1997, p. 382).

It is little wonder then that questions about the state's inaction should arise in the wake of a detailed examination of extreme social exclusion. People in the north inner city have asked hard questions and, for a long period, received few answers, less direction and almost no support. This lack of response on the part of the state led to anger. It is what Alphonso Lingis (1997) means when he speaks of anger as being a legitimate response, if not the most important political response to social exclusion. Quoting Jean-Luc Nancy, Lingis argues that anger in this instance concerns "the inadmissible, the intolerable" nature of exclusion and the profound distress people are made to carry as a result of their exclusion. That anger was evident during the period of the anti-drugs marches in the north inner city. It was expressed by the ICON member, quoted in Chapter One, who feared that wider social reactions to the problems of the north inner city could end by marginalising drug users and their families further, with the state trying to "keep a lid" on the extent of this local crisis so that its effects did not spill elsewhere (see Loughran, 1999, p. 309). A sense of anger, frustration and powerlessness was frequently expressed by the women who participated in this research. In Chapter Six, for example, women in a family support group stated their convictions that their work was not recognised at government level, that their very existence went unnoticed, and that the circumstances which were part of their daily lives as a result of heroin addiction in their families were of no concern to the government.

This real fear of not being heard is central to the experience of social exclusion and it represents one aspect of what Zygmunt Bauman (1998, pp. 46–50) terms a cessation of the "active" or "political citizenship" that was once seen as an integral contribution of the welfare state. Some policymakers in the twentieth century at least signed up to the idea that a "decent and dignified life" was there for every citizen, whether they could work or not. Bauman points out the many overlapping meanings that were attached to the notion of the welfare state — the vision that there could be universal benefits — was based on the universal acceptance of a work ethic, *because work was there.* Hence there was the assumption that a person would not become a second-class citizen when needing to use state benefits for such a need would only ever be a temporary one in relation to a temporary loss of work. However, de-industrialisation, long-term unemployment and the accompanying moves to downsize the welfare state ended that vision of a "dignified life".

Bauman argues that when work is no longer there, except for the more highly trained and highly skilled operatives in an increasingly technological society, those who cannot work at that level are not only pushed to the margins and silenced; their reliance on state welfare places them in a precarious political position for they are seen as second-class citizens.[1] Full political citizenship

---

[1] Wacquant (1993) and Bourgois (1997) argue that those who are subject to this stripping away of dignity more often than not end by accepting that definition of

vanishes when paid work itself vanishes and with it the role work has played in achieving social integration for individuals and their families. Those who do not work become aberrations from the social norm, even more so when the problem of widespread illegal drug use enters this scene. As traditional industrial jobs are shed and much work is relocated to cheaper sites in Third World countries,[2] the state becomes an uncertain buffer between those who face permanent exclusion from the now highly technologised labour market and a wider society which has less commitment than ever to maintaining the welfare state.

The capacity of a state to disengage from the excluded, who have endured their exclusion without any choice or control over their fate, is considerable. The trend towards this is most apparent in the United States where, as Phillipe Bourgois (1997) has observed:

> Self-destructive addiction is merely the medium for desperate people to internalise their frustration, resistance and powerlessness. . . . The problem of substance abuse in the United States is worse in the 1990s . . . because of a polarization of the structural roots that generate self-destructive behaviour and criminal activity. The economic base of the traditional working class has eroded. . . . Greater proportions of the population are being socially marginalized. The restructuring of the world economy by multinational corporations . . . as well as the exhaustion of social democratic models for public sector intervention on behalf of the poor, have escalated inequalities around class, ethnicity and gender (Bourgois, 1997, p. 319).

---

themselves. In the context of Dublin's north inner city, people describe how they have to live with the definition of themselves as "scum" if heroin addiction is present.

[2] Bauman (1998: p. 52–53) points out that maintaining international competitiveness now relies on the shedding of expensive labour which is less necessary than ever to carry on production in increasingly automated industries in developed countries, and having the speed and autonomy, when operations still demand human labour, to relocate to cheaper settings outside western welfare states. The importance of this level of control can be measured by the huge rewards that are made to corporate heads who accomplish these movements.

If it is possible to speak of good fortune in the same breath as marginalisation, the luck of the Irish situation is that we have not yet
moved along the road towards the scenario described by Bourgois,
towards the total scaling down of the state's involvement in all but
the most basic services. At present, Ireland is influenced by the
major impetus of the EU development programmes in trying to
overcome the worst effects of marginalisation and exclusion. The
overall logic is that investment in job creation and enterprise
strategies based at local level, along with community development, will hold back, at least temporarily, the numbers of the "new
poor" (Bauman, 1998). Translated to local level in the north inner
city, this is about trying to reduce the 59 per cent unemployment
rate that obtained in Mountjoy A Ward in 2000.

Curtin and Varley (1997, p. 383) note that a shift in the EU
anti-poverty programmes towards area-based development from
the late 1980s onwards introduced the concepts of equity, partnership and participation into state policies and enabled localities defined by their social exclusion to achieve a relatively high profile
on the social policy agenda. Certainly it is higher than might be
thought politically feasible in the move towards a globalised economy with all the attendant damages that Bauman, Bourgois, Wacquant and Lingis record.

In the next section of this chapter, I want to highlight some of
the possibilities and changes that this sectoral development work
has opened up for the north inner city, especially since the mid-
1990s, as well as discussing some of the recent shifts in drugs policies which have begun to respond to the social contexts of heroin
use. However, as encouraging as this work is, there remain tensions and major gaps, many of them with specific consequences
for women, and especially for women as mothers. And, because
this project has as its special focus an examination of women's
multiple roles and positions in the north inner city community,
including their work for and within the community, I explore
where women remain marginalised and less heard, basing my discussion on the findings from the previous three chapters. Finally, I
discuss strategies for increasing women's participation and decision-making in their communities as a contribution to help re-
build these communities in the wake of all they have undergone.
Whether or not this sectoral development work — with its empha-

sis on a partnership strategy — represents a temporary reprieve only is not as important, I believe, as is the work of building new modes of participation and engagement in the north inner city.

RECENT STATE AND VOLUNTARY INITIATIVES

Local Employment

The impetus of the EU Poverty Three programmes led the state into a partnership approach. Even if this was an instrumentalist approach in response to available funding (Curtin and Varley, 1997, p. 387), the programmes and finance on such an expanded scale opened up a new field of operations for the community sector in Ireland. The 1991–1993 PESP government programme spoke of these partnerships as being driven by a "bottom-up" and integrated approach. However inadequately understood or recognised by government departments, this approach became firmly embedded in the Local Development Programme which was part of the National Development Plan, 1994–1999. The establishment of Area Development Management Limited (ADM), the associated local partnership companies, the national anti-poverty strategy and the continued emphasis on the need to develop specific interventions for urban areas with high measures of disadvantage, including long-term unemployment, indicate that the Irish government is committed to this area of work for the foreseeable future.

There are critics of the government's approach and of the fact that community partnership areas may have been set an impossible mission: of creating opportunities for employment where the sustainability of such job creation is highly questionable. But as Varley (1998, p. 404) has noted, empowerment can ebb and flow "in response to a large number of contingent circumstances". For the present at least, what matters is that there are opportunities to push a strong local agenda for the north inner city. There are two organisations which have been centrally involved in this work. One is the Dublin Inner City Partnership (DICP) and the second is ICON, the area network for the northeast quadrant of the north inner city.

The DICP, having begun its work in 1991, has concentrated on reducing the burden of long-term unemployment through the establishment of a local employment service, direct support for new enterprises, supporting the Whole-time Jobs Initiative that has enabled long-term unemployed people to sign off the Live Register, and pre-training, retraining and education initiatives. It has also actively worked on the issue of expanding the range of community-based childcare services,[3] supporting community-based arts, and assisting local environmental improvements. The DICP has also worked to support local area networks in their bids to obtain redevelopment and refurbished housing, based on people's needs and choices with its Strategic Action Plans (DICP, 1999). This is a complex, holistic approach intent on resourcing local communities in ways which respect their dignity and the scope of their considerable expertise. It is also dependent on the state for its funding and continued commitment. So there is an outstanding need to sustain political agency on the issue of social exclusion against the weight of equally complex national and international agendas, where resolving social exclusion may not attract continuing political support in the future from other, far more powerful players.

ICON is a network of community groups in the northeast inner city which has its genesis in the many community efforts from the 1970s to organise locally and to contest and lobby nationally about the ongoing crisis of social exclusion. ICON has identified a core problem of the lack of "effective representation of community groups in the area" (ICON, 1999, p. 2) and has been especially concerned about the need for local representation on the Dublin Docklands Development Authority, a quango charged with redevelopment of the abandoned docks area at the end of the 1980s. The initial establishment of the Irish Financial Services Centre in the area had brought no economic or social value into the lives of the immediate communities and the 1997 publication of a £1.6 (€2.03) billion Docklands Development Plan for construction of commercial service facilities and private residential property over a 15-year period, brought demands from ICON for a local labour clause, for re-training and targeting of specific job opportunities

---

[3] The recently set up County Childcare Committee can be expected to develop its own action plans in due course to deal with this pressing issue.

emerging from the redeveloped complex so that people from the original inner city community could derive some real benefit.

ICON obtained local community representation on the Dublin Docklands Authority Council. It also obtained a local labour clause of 20 per cent as part of the redevelopment plan. This was fulfilled, but the skilled and long-term nature of this work has needed negotiation. This is because there are fewer and fewer jobs at the level of general operatives, and the technology of the construction industry is changing to the extent that workers now need literacy, and even computer literacy, if they are to have a future. An example of this is the construction of the new bank complex at the entrance to Commons Street. Because cement is no longer mixed on site but is driven in as ready-mixed batches, and because windows are pre-assembled elsewhere and also driven in, only one person was needed on site as a general unskilled operative (personal communication, Peter Nolan, ICES). Thus, technology outreach (and the kind of interventions and training required to relocate those who are long-term unemployed) has posed a huge challenge in trying to meet the local labour clause.

ICON has pinpointed the need for training to be linked directly to "local labour market requirements" (ICON, 1999, p. 7). They have also invested considerable energy in promoting the "social economy" which they define as an "economy moulded by local communities out of resources available to them" (ibid.). Another definition of the social economy comes from the Alliance for Work Forum, part of ICON, which ran a seminar on the social economy in 1996, investigating its potential to create new jobs at local level which local people could fill while meeting urgent local community development needs in areas like the provision of childcare, youth and sports provision, community work and drugs support work. The concept coming from the EU seemed to fit into the local agenda of "social service provision at a local level by local actors" (Rush, 1997, p. 3). Rush, however, cautioned that there were different interpretations about the mechanisms and meanings of the social economy. If labour market policy analysts saw it as a "quick-fix" for unemployment and therefore tried to align this development with traditional labour market measures of competitiveness and so on, the sector would die on its feet as a "second class economy".

Some of these tensions are apparent in the report of the Social Economy Working Group which was published in 1998. Set up as part of the government Partnership 2000 review, its remit was to examine the potential of the social economy, along with appropriate support mechanisms (Social Economy Working Group, 1998). The report commented that the evolving social economy was beginning to play a significant part in communities where there is extreme social disadvantage, but that it was being mediated through funding mechanisms which were not "directly designed for its needs" (ibid., pp. 8–9). Its "dynamism" was validated and the fact that it was working from a "bottom-up approach" (ibid., p. 55). The group recommended that a Social Economy Programme should be implemented with a re-allocation of existing resources around job creation and an adaptation of the Community Employment Scheme and other programmes. The establishment of a social economy was defined as a "policy objective" in its own right and not the "secondary" outcome of other policies and programmes devoted to labour market measures.

However, since the publication of that report, the problems of interpretation over these fledgling efforts have mushroomed. The Working Group itself stated that the development of a formal programme must not be seen to impinge on or impede in any way the labour supply for the "open market" but the group did accept that "a proportion of long-term unemployed persons may realistically never be able to access the open market" (ibid., p. 52). The debate and disagreement that has hung over short-term temporary employment schemes since the 1980s centres on the problem of translating short-term job schemes, which are often viable for the participants only because secondary social welfare benefits accompany them, into waged work with a progression route into the open labour market.

Despite the personal and local importance of these schemes, a key report on the Community Employment Scheme by the consultants Deloitte and Touche for the Department of Enterprise and Employment in 1998 recommended cutting the CE programme drastically. The Whole-time Jobs Initiative was also evaluated and again the issue of progression routes from assisted labour market programmes arose. The cuts and changes in eligibility for CE places which were subsequently announced by the

Tánaiste, Mary Harney, raised objections around the country. For the inner city, the DICP pointed out that CE, for all its drawbacks as a stopgap, was the only device protecting lone parents, who comprised 42 per cent of CE participants in the inner city, from an even harder economic situation than they already faced. Therefore, until the Social Economy programme could be established with "substitute social economy positions", it was "inconsistent" for the government to announce these cuts (DICP Press Release, 28 July 1999).

The language used here is critical to the differences in interpretation about the economy and therefore ultimately about the position of the state in mediating the futures of those who are socially excluded. The DICP language of "substitute social economy positions" may be closer to the reality of the problem of long-term sustainability of work. The government working group report on the social economy, on the other hand, appears to be caught between the need to service the market economy — the report speaks of a "movement over time" towards "commercial viability" as a potential advantage of pursuing a social economy package along with the advantage of providing "an expanded market for goods and services" (Social Economy Working Group, 1998, pp. 28–29) — and the recognition that certain enterprises in disadvantaged areas, while necessary, may not be commercially viable (ibid.).

There is a pressure to conform to strict marketplace definitions which inevitably focus on increasing competitiveness while reducing the welfare state. Thus, a recent OECD study (Sabel, 1996) argues that the area-based management approach enables the Irish partnerships to construct "a system of effective local adjustment precisely by helping to integrate efforts to improve the competitiveness of firms to increase the employability of residents in the local community" (ibid., p. 43) while limiting "the provision of anything like comprehensive social insurance to the most vulnerable groups — the poor and the unemployed" (ibid.).[4] This perspective, while not appearing to account at all for the social impact on a European workforce which contributes to an improved com-

---

[4] These issues are also addressed in the proceedings from a conference on the Social Economy in Ireland, in Galway. See Area Development Management (1998).

petitive edge by becoming increasingly "flexible",[5] is also likely to be at odds with the locally articulated needs, complexities and entrenched problems of employability which have resulted from decades of neglect and which the work of the DICP and ICON seek to redress. In the context of earlier partnership work, Curtin and Varley (1997, p. 390) have noted that "dark shadows can be cast by the wider environment on the work of the anti-poverty partnerships" when the state is asked by communities to exercise its powerful agency by intervening on behalf of the socially excluded and yet is also reducing its commitments in other strategic areas. This is where there is a disquieting sense of how long the Irish state can hold what is an essentially ambiguous and contradictory buffer position. Bourgois (1997) has spoken about the need for "political will" to end urban crisis. But from the perspectives of communities like the north inner city, the problem of sustaining that political will urgently needs debate. Such a debate also urgently needs to incorporate the lived realities of communities still struggling with heroin. Urban regeneration, like the Integrated Area Plan for the north east inner city developed by Dublin Corporation are less likely to succeed, if attention is not paid to how heroin has changed the fabric of the communities so affected, and perhaps most crucially to the problem of developing community participation and process.

Drugs Policies

Many of the significant recommendations that resulted in changes to national drugs policies from 1996 arose as a result of experiences and efforts by the community sector in the north inner city. The state had to acknowledge that drug use and drug addiction could not be dealt with by deploying limited resources to deal with treatment issues on the one hand, and on the other, consider

---

[5] This labour flexibility, in line with what the head of the International Monetary Fund, Michel Camdessus, terms the "methodical liberalisation of capital movements" (*Le Monde*, 24 April 1998), led in 1997 alone to "in just ten days, three European firms cut[ting] jobs on a scale large enough to be compared with the numbers mentioned in the new French and British governments' proposals on job creation" (M. Woollacott, "Bosses must learn to behave better again", *Guardian*, 14 June 1997).

drugs a problem of law enforcement, in line with the rhetoric about the "war on drugs" (Murphy, 1996). Instead, the two Ministerial Task Force reports on drugs of 1996 and 1997 (Department of the Taoiseach, Task Force, 1996; 1997) paid attention as never before to the connections between areas of extreme disadvantage and the strength of the illegal drug culture in those areas. The First Task Force report, in recommending the setting up of a national–local partnership approach and the institution of local drugs task forces, drew heavily on the model of organisation which had been instituted in the Inter-Agency Drugs Project set up by ICON. This worked through a series of sub-committees or core teams to create specific agendas on prevention, treatment and supply reduction and, most importantly, through representation on these sub-committees, the community had a direct input into local policy development.

In addition to ensuring that special local treatment programmes were set up for heroin smokers, ICON was also anxious to advance the work of a community support service for drug users and their families. This service sought to offer information, advice, referral, initial counselling and an after-hours service. These elements, combined with having a local community worker trained in drugs and support issues, appeared invaluable and at a number of points in the fieldwork for this project, this service was cited as very important in the lives of women trying to cope with their children.

But what is most important is that it was a locally identified need which the local task force could respond to in the way that made most sense for the north inner city community. On the basis of a formal evaluation (McCarthy, 1999), ICON has strongly argued the case for this type of service being built into local responses elsewhere. Interestingly, however, ICON notes that efforts to build liaison between the statutory health authority services and this community support service at local level have been "frustrating" because, ICON argues, there is a "lack of understanding by Eastern Health Board workers of the importance of the community sector and of community development processes" (ICON, 1999, p. 14). The problem remains that, without this kind of process, local responses to drug use will not be integrated into the realities of how the community is living with illegal drug use. The expectations of the statutory sector that somehow people "cope" is belied by the use made of the community support service.

As ICON currently read the situation, their concerns focus not just on heroin use but on the changing trends towards multiple drug use, which has become part of the street scene, with prescription drugs and illegal supplies of methadone available. They are clear that street dealing has not gone from the area, just that it is less evident than it was before the campaigns of the mid-1990s. The local statutory drugs treatment services should be able to track and respond to these changes, but they will require both the information and the communication at local level which can alert them to these differences. This points again to the fundamental issue of locating illegal drug use in its social context, and ensuring that strategies stem from the community's realities. ICON acknowledge that the street campaign was a "difficult" undertaking for them and that a different approach is now required. In its recent action plan, ICON emphasised again the necessity for integrated action:

> The issues of economic development, education, drugs and family and community support are all interlinked. Unless the last three are addressed, the economic developments are unlikely to benefit local people as they should (1999, p. 7).

Some sense of this need for integrated action on drugs comes through the Second Ministerial Task Force, where the changing nature of drug use as part of young people's perceived recreational needs was picked up. The Task Force noted that the use of cannabis and ecstasy is now a nation-wide phenomenon. But the Task Force also stated that a "just say no" campaign to drugs was likely to prove ineffective and that young people need factual information on the known dangers of drugs, as well as practical advice on using drugs, despite the known dangers (Second Ministerial Task Force, 1997, p. 45).

Observing and responding to the many issues that continue to bedevil life in the north inner city due to illegal drug use and all its related problems, the Inter-Agency Drugs Project/North Inner City Drugs Task Force has focused on an integrated strategy from the outset. It has built into its work a system of representation which weights the community itself as a serious player with vital experience. Six community representatives and one drug service user representative are part of the NICDTF structure. And with an anticipated budget of just over €1,000,000 to help fund its current strategic plan, the NICDTF has highlighted 14 key issues arising from the first phase of its work about which it has set out objectives for its second phase (NICDTF, 2001, p. 7). Over an 18-month period, a series of public meetings, seminars, meetings with local projects and follow-up meetings were held to first help identify and then to clarify its strategic objectives. Not surprisingly, in the course of that extensive consultation process, some of the same issues raised by the women were identified. Education and childcare, for example, were seen as key issues in most initiatives while many groups also reported difficulty in engaging in particular with the Department of Education. There were calls for more collaboration at senior level between government departments and agencies when local services were being planned and the task of sustaining community participation was seen as indivisible from the work of designing and delivering programmes of action in the north inner city (ibid.) The need for long-term training and employment for former users was also reiterated. The million euros allocated to the North Inner City Drugs Task Force for its second phase of work will be badly needed to sustain and extend the work it has already undertaken to support and that which it hopes to expand on in the future.

The national evaluation of local drugs task force projects also picks up on some of the concerns and themes explored in the course of this study (Ruddle et al., 2000). The evaluation findings indicated the importance of the community's involvement in order for projects to successfully achieve their objectives. But the authors argue that communities must have confidence in the nature of the projects undertaken in order to secure their involvement and that shows up the need for both effective representation by the community and capacity building to secure participation long term (ibid., pp. 95–96). Resource issues, including long-term funding, staffing and premises were identified by many projects as critical issues if they were to be enabled to maintain and improve their services.

Long before this evaluation got under way, Loughran (1999, p. 327) raised concerns that the location of the drugs issues at governmental level rolled back some of the impact of the Task Force reports. The Department of Tourism, Sport and Recreation, she contended, is not a "high-status" department, whereas the integrated social and economic approach needed to respond comprehensively to the drugs issue requires heavy-duty governmental resources and expertise. She struck a worrying note when she declared that:

> a difficult balance must be struck between responding to the demands of voters at large to control the drugs problem, while attempting to respond in a responsible way to the needs of drug users and their families (ibid.).

Another way of stating that logic is that the majority of the voting population which has not been subject to the devastating experience of social exclusion and illegal drugs sees no special value in responding comprehensively to how those problems arose. This majority has the voting power to deny that comprehensive and costly approach to marginalised communities, having never experienced the personal and social costs of exclusion. Both the new strategic plan for the north inner city on behalf of the NICDTF and the national evaluation point up the essential requirement of an integrated approach. The women in the course of this study have observed that heroin is not going to go away as a problem. Clearly the government has got this message, as reflected in the recently published strategy document, *Building on Experience – National Drugs Strategy 2001–2008* (National Drugs Strategy Unit, 2001). One objective of the long-term strategy is "to reduce the harm caused by drug misuse to individuals, families and communities" (ibid.). But the costs of responses to underpin this objective are going to be very long-term costs. The question is whether there will be the political resolve in the long-term to provide the vital resources for this work.

AN INCOMPLETE AGENDA: SOCIAL EXCLUSION FROM WOMEN'S PERSPECTIVES

On the basis of heroin users' experiences, a recommendation was made at the conclusion of the sister project to this one, that more use be made of Section 28.2 of the 1977 Misuse of Drugs Act, which would permit the Courts to direct offenders to treatment facilities rather than to prison (Coveney et al., 1999). Many people involved with drug treatment and support services have called for this kind of intervention and in April 2000, it was announced by the Minister of State with Responsibility for the National Drugs Strategy at a European Cities Against Drugs conference that was held in Dublin, that this would be offered to non-violent offenders who are brought before the courts. The Minister stated that a judicial order of compulsory rehabilitation could prove a successful strategy for drug users anxious to tackle their addiction. Additionally, the Minister said:

> In these cases, family support is very, very important for people trying to get off drugs and rehabilitate themselves. ("Rehab now officially part of drug recovery", *Irish Independent*, 29 April 2000)

This marked the beginning of a change of policy in drugs sentencing (although there are difficulties around enforced rehabilitation — a similar scheme in the Netherlands uses a contract based between the police and the offender — see Coveney et al., 1999).

But it was the reference to family support that is striking in the context of this study. It is explicit recognition from the state that drug users need family support. Yet there was no hint by the Minister of the support work which is vital for the families, and for the women who by and large will be the linchpins of that family support, in order for this new initiative to work.

A pilot Drugs Court, operating at district court level for non-violent drugs-related offences, has since been set up, where treatment may be imposed instead of a prison sentence. The question is whether this additional context of family-related support issues can be built into its work.

In the course of this ethnographic study, women have carefully articulated why they continue with their care and support of children who are users, but where they must learn to put boundaries around that work for their own sakes and for the sake of the rest of their family. What women have also stated in these pages is that there is no viable way that family support can be offered to drug users seeking rehabilitation, if the families themselves do not have support mechanisms to help them cope with the emotional, practical and financial burdens that responding to a drug user entails. Moreover, if statutory support for the user is not connected to long-term rehabilitation in respect of self-identity, education and training, family support is likely to be insufficient to help the user.

What will happen in this case if the Minister, his officials, and the judiciary remain uninformed about the fact, for example, that drug users can go through hundreds of "detoxes" unsuccessfully; or that families can suffer deep disruption in the course of this, as indicated in Chapter Four, and may be forced to withdraw support; or even that excellent support at the right time, from the family and from the community, can result in a successful turning away from heroin use? The problem is not just that of unpredictability of outcome; it is that to achieve a good outcome on this front, what will be required is a truly integrated effort, recognised and supported by the state from the outset *or this important shift in policy will fail.*

In the course of this ethnography, we have encountered an impressive range of active strategies that women are employing on a number of fronts to assist them, their families and their communities through the crisis of heroin, where it has been both symbol and symptom of exclusion and marginalisation. Following on from where they have built up or contributed to these strategies, women have offered tightly structured analyses about the following resource needs to enable this work to go further, needs which the women themselves cannot fulfil.

Group I — Strengthening Individual Capacities

- Access to and funding for second chance education for women, including re-training and accreditation
- Access to affordable quality childcare to enable women to participate in re-training and second-chance education

- Building long-term progression routes into skilled work for women, including teaching, youth and community work, counselling and facilitation and childcare work

- Access to personal development, second-chance education and relevant retraining programmes for older men in inner city communities

- Creation of formal programmes for teaching assistants and points of entry to teacher-training programmes for older people from the inner city

- Models of best practice to deal with gender-proofing of the statutory and voluntary sectors working in the inner city to remove any remaining "glass ceilings".

Group II — Strengthening Community Capacities

- Access to and funding for training to build community capacity on decision-making and consensus at local level, including training in the running of consensus conferences

- Access to and funding for training to build community negotiating capacity with the state and with private enterprise about the future development of the north inner city

- Relevant, funded local structures to achieve partnership in decision-making on estate management and regeneration

- A sensitive and multi-faceted policy developed by both Dublin City Council (formerly Dublin Corporation) and local estate management groups on the problem of responding to anti-social behaviour in houses and flats, including the problem of drug-dealing

- Consistent and responsible community Garda presence to control street-selling of illegal drugs.

Group III — Measures for Drug Users

- Long-term personal and social reintegration community-based programmes for drug users in treatment

- Immediate bridging social welfare payments for drug offenders just released from prison

- Access to and funding for second-chance education including re-training, accreditation and long-term progression routes into skilled work for former drug users.

Group IV — Ensuring the Growth of Child and Youth-Centred Facilities

- Consistent long-term funding and back-up resources for community prevention of drug use and support work, including summer projects, youth clubs, after-school clubs and sports clubs

- Relevant drugs education and life-skills programmes in primary and second-level schools.

Group V — Responding to Parents in Need

- Consistent long-term funding, back-up resources and training for counselling and family support work

- Establishment of support programmes in the community for younger mothers

- Relevant and accessible drugs education and life-skills programmes for parents in the community.

Women are trying to resolve aspects of their social exclusion but their active agency in doing so is still limited by their lack of structural power and support. This is why they speak as they do in Chapter Six, that there is "no one out there who is going to help" and of having to "get together and fight for their rights" for themselves and their families. Of course, there are many more women who are dealing at a personal level with the strains and challenges of living with the threat of heroin to their families who are not yet involved at group or community level and who may even feel actively excluded from that kind of participation.

In general terms, Irish society still imposes many "glass ceilings" which prevent women's active participation and problem-solving from being translated into decision-making positions. While Pat O'Connor (1998, pp. 247–253) rightly identifies the increased visibility of women in working class communities, she also presents convincing evidence that women's entry into public arenas is limited because the arenas themselves have not changed substantively, because the organisational culture remains effectively masculine and exclusive. The specific and continuing problems faced by women —

- low-paid, unskilled work

- lack of childcare

- lack of sufficient and adequate second-chance education and accreditation

- barriers to active labour market measures for married women

- poverty for lone parents

— resonate even more strongly in communities hard hit by heroin.

At local levels, these issues constitute rigid "glass ceilings"; insufficient structural response to these issues and to the value of what O'Connor defines as "the sheer extent of women's contribution to the family and community" (ibid.) is preventing a range of energetic actors — women who have already taken real risks and worked unremittingly — from implementing the long-term changes which are vital if communities are to be brought through the experiences of living with heroin.

The strong case which women in this study have made for sustained long-term funding by the state of locally managed work which builds expertise in the community seems unassailably correct. How then will women make their voices count? How is their exercise of "active citizenship" in the work they have done and are doing for themselves, their families and in their communities to be truly sustained and matched by the state?

Women's Work in Achieving Political Change: Strategies for Participation

Illegal drug use centred on a heroin culture continues to be part of the context for the north inner city and shows no sign of abating in the near future. The north inner city also continues to exhibit high rates of deprivation, despite the so-called "Celtic Tiger" economy.[6]

As this ethnography amply demonstrates, women will continue to be principal agents trying to cope at family level with the distressing circumstances created by heroin use. Their caring work creates a social counterweight to the unacceptable burdens of heroin use in marginalised communities. The women who contributed to this study are arguably fortunate, marked by their energy and commitment in the wake of their difficulties to use those extreme and difficult experiences as a basis of understanding to bring about change in their community. Three questions stem from this:

1. How can the women who have had less energy or support but the same range of problems be identified and better supported?

2. How can women's caring work with their families and communities become politically validated?

3. How can women as a whole in the north inner city have their caring work matched in resources, commitment and energy by the state?

Melissa Benn, writing recently on the need for a new politics of motherhood, has argued in the British context that the "vocabulary of the market has seeped into everything, falsely opposed at every turn to the language of the state, when the real dichotomy is surely between a willingness to challenge or underwrite inequality". Benn is deeply concerned about the "need to create a new respect about caring work":

---

[6] It is worth referring here to Pat O'Connor's analysis that the "Celtic Tiger" has been built substantially on women's labour force participation but that the major portion of women's paid work continues to be low-paid, part-time and less-skilled, while women's caring work in the home goes unacknowledged (O'Connor, 1998).

> The poorest mothers will not get the help they need if we do
> not call a halt to the "what is mine, is mine" society (1998,
> p. 252).

Benn argues that the widely accepted view that mothering is positive neatly gets society out of providing any support for women as
mothers. Similarly, Pat O'Connor points out that there is a growing number of studies which indicate how demanding caring work
is, especially the caring and rearing of children. But the Irish state,
she argues, only becomes interested in children, teenagers or
young adults when they fulfil certain criteria of being "at risk", and
not beforehand. Thus, until that point is reached, the state is not
particularly challenged to provide support, let alone support for
women in the most marginalised circumstances.

This is not to say that the Irish state has not begun to respond
on the issue of gender, but there is a very long way to go. The new
National Development Plan does incorporate women's issues
through an intent to "gender mainstreaming" in that all government decisions are now required to set out their impact on
women. The government-funded initiative on the social economy
has women's interests represented within the Department of Enterprise and Employment by the National Women's Council of Ireland. Ursula Barry points out that, at Local Area Partnership level,
women have been more involved in planning, enterprise development, training and community support activities (Barry, 1998, p.
358). But Barry also observes that the National Anti-Poverty Strategy has had no additional allocation of funds to help achieve
gender equality although it is one of the stated principles. And,
many of the initiatives have been "piecemeal" and "uneven". Barry
sees the need for a "strong and clear framework" for assessing
changes and for setting benchmarks on what needs remain unmet
(ibid, p. 359).

My concern is that any worthwhile impact assessment needs to
be very strongly directed from the women who are most immediately affected by social exclusion. Representation by the National
Women's Council on the Social Economy Committee, for example,
does not show that the state is choosing to include directly in the
decision-making process, those groups of women who live the
realities of social exclusion. What the women's accounts presented

in this study show is that there is a gap and a deficit between their work and where the state picks up on the problems of social exclusion, especially the version experienced by women. Their "active citizenship" has not been met and matched by the state in all its recent initiatives.[7] Much more remains to be done by the state to match their creativity in developing democratic and supportive processes at local level. Of course, there are many more clamorous and politically powerful voices seeking the state's attention, and indeed it is argued that the state is a weak actor amidst this globalising clamour.

In the attempt to retrieve citizenship as "enabling power", Zygmunt Bauman has explored the need to restore a "public/private space", not the private household and not the state, but a space where the meaning of the "common good" and all its myriad differences can be debated, where "private worries" from everyday life become "public issues" (Bauman, 1999). "Private worries" over open drug-dealing in the community led to the "public issue" of a street campaign in the north inner city in 1996. If there had been a different kind of listening taking place, if there had been that sort of public/private space with/between the citizens and the state, those actions would have been rendered unnecessary because what had become ordinary everyday life for the north inner city community would have been aired as intolerable for citizens. But there was no such space.

The sociologist David Byrne writes of the "creative capacity of human beings as reflexive and understanding actors and doers" (Byrne, 1998, p. 43). This has to be the starting point for the construction of a public/private space where the state is listening to the expertise of women in their locality of the north inner city.

---

[7] The issue of whether more extended initiatives are "affordable" by the state is a debate which urgently needs to be recast. Bauman (1998: p, 185–6) argues that affordability is tied to the idea that those who work pay the state their taxes so that social measures are a transfer from those who work to those who do not work. The extreme illogic of this argument in a global setting, where there has not been a positive relationship between productivity and the size of the labour force since the end of the 1960s, is one which needs to be explored in relation to the Celtic Tiger economy's continuance. The existence of first and second-class citizens, those who work and pay and those who do not, could be readily disassembled by the institution of a basic income. For arguments on the basic income in an Irish context, see Reynolds and Healy (1994).

Byrne's arguments on the complexity of local social systems indicate that, although there is no linear law which says that this programme will accomplish this end, nonetheless an analysis of a possible set of desired outcomes can help in the identification of interventions to achieve those outcomes. This is the work of agency and decision-making which should be part of active citizenship.

Take just one example of this. Education and re-training are seen as essential to overcoming the attraction of the heroin culture by providing a strong alternative identity for teenagers and young adults.[8] In this study, women discussed doing work as classroom assistants in the schools and running clubs after school where homework could be done. They also discussed the value they are putting on education and the hope that their own efforts to obtain second-chance education will inspire their children to value education. Much research has already examined the fact that individual academic achievement relies on a school and peer-group culture which values that achievement (see footnote 6, Chapter One, page 12). So the obvious policy move is to redefine the educational resource pool as widely as possible, and thus to support and equip local women who are now working as teacher assistants to become fully qualified teachers in their own right, able to work and teach in their own community.

Women have themselves identified the potential of this movement. On this matter, as with others, they have pointed out that they are rational experts very capable of developing the "strong social programme" (Byrne, 1998, p. 118) which is vital for the future of the inner city. But for women to be able to prioritise their analyses, to knit these together into a positive series of strategies, we need to develop what Rachel Iredale is discussing: "a decision-making culture that is both evidence-based and inclusive" (Iredale, 1999, p. 183). She cites the growing trend towards "qualitative research with

---

[8] I state this fully aware of the overwhelming evidence on the declining workbase globally. But I am also arguing that the Irish state could make different decisions about work and its citizens, such as a shift in the social structure stemming from the establishment of a basic income, which could open the routes in the future, after the "Celtic Tiger" economy has gone its way, to senses of self-worth and citizenship for everyone here, despite a changed economic context.

ordinary members of the public". She also cites the development of democratic forums, like "planning cells", used in Germany and "consensus conferences" used in Denmark, where the expertise of citizens in their ordinary lives and the expertise of professionals are brought together in working groups over a limited period (of, say, one week) to assess and hammer out solutions for social problems, including aspects of urban renewal and so on. An important example of this closer to home may lie in the work of the Women's Coalition in Northern Ireland; here a group worked to come together and establish consensus over critical social and local political issues, while at the same time recognising the depth of the conflict that separated many of its members from one another.

There are two points here. The first is that many problems are seen as resolvable if there is a mechanism to bring together the relevant players and expertises. Their conclusions can then be channelled into the policy-making process, which can be further validated by parliamentary debate in its usual forms as new policies are put out for approval by the legislature. The second point is that genuinely participatory democratic processes like these strengthen communities.

What if the state, through its many emerging mechanisms of local partnership and so on, were to facilitate women in the north inner city in this way to emerge with an explicit social programme that can deal with their stated concerns as listed above? Women in the north inner city already have the blueprint for their futures. If women are skilled, resourced and in place, the community will benefit and change.

Summary of Chapter Seven

♦ *In this chapter, the themes developed in the previous chapters are brought together, first examining the problem of social exclusion from the perspective of the lack of democratic participation and representation.*

♦ *The women in the north inner city who participated in this study have expressed anger, frustration and powerlessness over the lack of sufficient response from the state about the heroin culture, long-term unemployment, and other aspects of social exclusion which they live with on a daily basis. Using the work of the sociologist, Zygmunt Bauman, it is argued that women and their families in the north inner city, as a result of no longer having paid employment and the dignity that work gives to people, have effectively lost full political citizenship; their voices have counted less because, living at the epicentre of a huge series of overlapping problems, including heroin, they are largely dependent on social welfare and cannot command the resources necessary to address these problems. Thus it is argued that the state is an uncertain buffer caught between those who are permanently excluded from the labour market unless they can gain skills and the shrinkage of the welfare state under demands for increasing competitiveness.*

◆ *Efforts by the state, with EU backing, to develop local employment initiatives are discussed; using this leverage, the Dublin Inner City Partnership and ICON are both pushing to achieve a strong local agenda that reflects local labour market needs. The tensions, however, between local needs and state support to service these, and arguments which favour a market-driven approach, emerge in recent work on the potential for the social economy. While recent review groups have seen the need to develop specific mechanisms for a social economy programme, thus abolishing the reliance on piecemeal short-term job creation schemes, the perceived good of a locally based social economy that is commercially viable may be difficult to achieve in the long term without state resources. Yet, if there is ongoing need for state expenditure to sustain such developments in the long-term, the political will to support this may not be there.*

◆ *In relation to changes in drugs policies, much of the impetus for evolving work at national level has come from the community sector in the north inner city. But an integrated approach to the drugs problem has to include the provision of education, long-term employment opportunities, and family and community support structures. Also, there is some concern about the long-term commitment of the state to this integrated approach, which is costly, and which may not meet the approval of the wider electorate who may remain unaware of the full impact of living in a marginalised community.*

♦ *The recent setting-up of a new pilot court project offering drugs rehabilitation rather than prison sentences to non-violent offenders before the courts for drugs-related crime provides a good example of a more integrated approach. This represents an important advance, especially if drug users can be counselled about their choices. But unless sufficient funding and long-term support structures are put in place for the drug users and their families, it is likely to fail.*

♦ *Relevant and accessible drugs education and life-skills programmes for parents in the community.*

♦ *Women have been energetic and creative actors in responding to problems at local level and have developed considerable expertise. But they continue to face "glass ceilings" because they are omitted from decision- and policy-making for the inner city. Yet they will remain the principal agents of family and community-building because of the caring work they do. Their active citizenship must be matched by the state in resources, energy and commitment. There is a need to create a politicised listening public/private space where the state can pick up on women's expertise.*

♦ *Tapping into women's expertise and problem-solving and increasing participation to build a strong social programme for the north inner city can be done through the institution of democratic forums like planning cells and consensus conferences, where women sit at local level with the expert policy-makers to develop a joint agenda.*

♦ *The recommendations coming out of this study stem from what the women themselves offered by way of concrete analyses of the needs in their communities for heroin users, for families, and for rebuilding the fabric of community life. Women are asking that their activism and caring work be met by comprehensive government action on the following:*

Group I — Strengthening Individual Capacities

♦ *Access to and funding for second-chance education for women, including re-training and accreditation*

♦ *Access to affordable quality childcare to enable women to participate in re-training and second-chance education*

♦ *Building long-term progression routes into skilled work for women, including teaching, youth and community work, counselling and facilitation and childcare work*

♦ *Access to personal development, second-chance education and relevant retraining programmes for older men in inner city communities*

♦ *Creation of formal programmes for teaching assistants and points of entry to teacher-training programmes for older people from the inner city*

♦ *Models of best practice to deal with gender-proofing of the statutory and voluntary sectors working in the inner city to remove any remaining "glass ceilings".*

Group II — Strengthening Community Capacities

♦ *Access to and funding for training to build community capacity on decision-making and consensus at local level, including training in the running of consensus conferences*

♦ *Access to and funding for training to build community negotiating capacity with the state and with private enterprise about the future development of the north inner city*

♦ *Relevant, funded local structures to achieve partnership in decision-making on estate management and regeneration*

♦ *A sensitive and multi-faceted policy developed by both Dublin City Council (formerly Dublin Corporation) and local estate management groups on the problem of responding to anti-social behaviour in houses and flats, including the problem of drug-dealing*

♦ *Consistent and responsible community Garda presence to control street selling of illegal drugs.*

Group III — Measures for Drug Users

♦ Long-term personal and social reintegration community-based programmes for drug users in treatment

♦ Immediate bridging social welfare payments for drug offenders just released from prison

♦ Access to and funding for second chance education including re-training, accreditation and long-term progression routes into skilled work for former drug users.

Group IV — Ensuring the Growth of Child and Youth-Centred Facilities

♦ Consistent long-term funding and back-up resources for community prevention of drug use and support work, including summer projects, youth clubs, after-school clubs and sports clubs

♦ Relevant drugs education and life-skills programmes in primary and second-level schools.

Group V — Responding to Parents in Need

♦ Consistent long-term funding, back-up resources and training for counselling and family support work

♦ Establishment of support programmes in the community for younger mothers.

BIBLIOGRAPHY

Adams, A. (1995), "Maternal Bonds: Recent Literature on Mothering", in *Signs*, Vol. 20, No. 2, pp. 414–427.

Area Development Management Ltd. (1998), *The Social Economy in Ireland: A perspective beyond 2000; Proceedings from a conference in Galway Bay Hotel, 17 November 1998*, Dublin: ADM Ltd.

Alliance for Work Forum (n.d.), *Profile of the North Inner City Community*, Dublin: AWF.

Ana Liffey Drug Project (1995), *Annual Report, 1994*, Dublin: ALDP.

Bacik, I. et al. (1998), "Crime and Poverty in Dublin", in I. Bacik and M. O'Connell (eds.), *Crime and Poverty in Ireland*, Dublin: Round Hall, Sweet and Maxwell.

Bannon, M. et al. (1981), *Urbanisation: problems of growth and decay in Dublin*, Dublin: NESC.

Barry, U. (1998), "Women, Equality and Public Policy", in S. Healy and B. Reynolds (eds.), *Social Policy in Ireland: Principles, Practice and Problems*, Dublin: Oak Tree Press.

Bauman, Z. (1990), *Thinking Sociologically*, Oxford: Blackwell.

Bauman, Z. (1998), *Work, Consumerism and the New Poor*, Milton Keynes: Open University.

Bauman, Z. (1999), *In Search of Politics*, London: Polity Press.

Behar, R. (1996), *The Vulnerable Observer: Anthropology that Breaks Your Heart*, Boston: Beacon Press.

Benn, M. (1998), *Madonna and Child: Towards a New Politics of Motherhood*, London: Jonathan Cape.

Blaxter, M. (1990), *Health and Lifestyles*, London: Routledge.

Bourgois, P. (1997), *In Search of Respect: Selling Crack in El Barrio*, Cambridge: Cambridge University Press.

Butler, S. (1991), "Drug Problems and Drug Policies in Ireland: A quarter of a century reviewed", in *Administration*, Vol. 39, No. 3.

Byrne, D. (1998), *Complexity Theory and the Social Sciences*, London: Routledge.

Carmody, P. and McEvoy, M. (1996), *A Study of Irish Female Prisoners*, Dublin: Stationery Office.

CityWide Drugs Crisis Campaign (1999), *Responding Together — The Crisis Continues*, Dublin: CDCC.

Clarke, J. (1990), "Mothers' Perceptions of the Needs and Resources of the An Lár Community: A Qualitative Analysis", Unpublished M.Sc. Thesis, Faculty of Medicine, University of Manchester.

Coakley, A. (1997), "Gendered Citizenship: The Social Construction of Mothers in Ireland", in A. Byrne and M. Leonard (eds.), *Women and Irish Society: A Sociological Reader*, Belfast: Beyond the Pale Publications.

Cockburn, C. (1998), *The Space Between Us: Negotiating Gender and National Identities in Conflict*, London: Zed Books.

Connolly, D. (1997), "Developing Dublin's Inner City — Who Benefits?" Unpublished M.Sc. Thesis, University of Dublin/Institute of Public Administration.

Connolly, L. (1997), "From Revolution to Devolution: Mapping the Contemporary Women's Movement in Ireland", in A. Byrne and M. Leonard (eds.), *Women and Irish Society: A Sociological Reader*, Belfast: Beyond the Pale Publications.

Coulter, C. (1993), *The Hidden Tradition: Feminism, Women and Nationalism*, Cork: Cork University Press.

Coveney, E. and Sheridan, S. (1996), "The Feminization of Power: Women's Agency in Inner City Dublin", Unpublished M. Phil. thesis, Centre for Women's Studies, Trinity College Dublin.

Coveney, E., Murphy-Lawless, J. and Sheridan, S. (1998a), *Women, Work and Family Responsibilities*, Dublin: Larkin Centre for the Unemployed/Combat Poverty Agency.

Coveney, E., Murphy-Lawless, J. and Sheridan, S. (1998b), *Barriers to Women's Access to Labour Market Measures*, Dublin: Department of Social, Community and Family Affairs.

Coveney, E, Murphy-Lawless, J., Redmond, D., and Sheridan, S. (1999), *Prevalence, Profiles and Policy: A case study of heroin drug use in inner city Dublin*, Dublin: North Inner City Drugs Task Force.

Curtin, C. and Varley, T. (1997), "Community Action and the State", in P. Clancy et al. (eds.), *Irish Society: Sociological Perspectives*, Dublin: IPA.

Daly, M. (1989), *Women and Poverty*, Dublin: Attic Press/Combat Poverty Agency.

Daly, M. (1993), "The Relationship between Women's Work and Poverty", in A. Smyth (ed.), *Irish Women's Studies Reader*, Dublin: Attic Press.

Dean, G. et al. (1983), *Drug Misuse in Ireland, 1982–1983: Investigation on a North Central Dublin Area and in Galway, Sligo and Cork*, Dublin: Medico-Social Research Board.

Di Quinzio, P. (1999), *The Impossibility of Motherhood: feminism, individualism, and the problem of mothering*, New York: Routledge.

Drudy, P. and McLaren, A. (1996), *Dublin: Economic and Social Trends Vol. 2*, Dublin: Trinity College Dublin.

Dublin Inner City Partnership (1999), *Sustaining Community Regeneration: Progress Report, 1997–1998*, Dublin: DICP.

Emerson, P.J. (1999), *From Belfast to the Balkans: Was "Democracy" Part of the Problem?* Belfast: The de Borda Institute.

Finch, J. (1984), "'It's Great to Have Someone to Talk To': The Ethics and Politics of Interviewing Women", in H. Roberts and C. Bell (eds.), *Social Researching: Politics, Problems and Practice*, London: Routledge and Kegan Paul.

Fine, M. (1994), "Working the Hyphens: Reinventing Self and Other in Qualitative Research", in Denzin, N. and Lincoln, Y. (eds.), *Handbook of Qualitative Research*, London: Sage.

Fitzgerald, E. and Ingoldsby, B. (1999), *Evaluation of the Employment Network and the Whole-time Job Initiative*, Dublin: DICP.

Ford, J. and Reutter, L. (1990), "Ethical dilemmas associated with small samples", in *Journal of Advanced Nursing*, 15, pp. 187–191.

Gamma (1998), "Dublin Inner City Partnership Area", Baseline Data Report, September, 1998, *Report No. 27*, Dublin: Area Development Management Limited.

Gorz, A. (1994), *Capitalism, Socialism, Ecology*, London: Verso.

Hogan, D. and Higgins, L. (2001), *When Parents Use Drugs: Key Findings from a Study of Children in the Care of Drug-using Parents*, Dublin: The Children's Centre, Trinity College Dublin.

ICN (1997), "Open Drug Dealing Resurfaces in Inner-City", in *Inner City News: Raising the Issues*, Vol. 10, No. 3, p. 2.

ICON (1994), *Grasping the Future: Inner City Organisations Network Area Action Plan for Dublin's North-East Inner City*, Dublin: ICON.

ICON (1999), *ICON Action Plan, 1999: The Next Step towards Inner City Renewal*, Dublin: ICON.

Iredale, R. (1999), "Public Consultation and Participation in Policy Making", in G. Kiely et al. (eds.), *Irish Social Policy in Context*, Dublin: University College Dublin Press.

Ireland, Department of the Taoiseach (1996), *First Report of the Ministerial Task Force on Measures to Reduce the Demand for Drugs*, Dublin: Stationery Office.

Ireland, Department of the Taoiseach (1997), *Second Report of the Ministerial Task Force on Measures to Reduce the Demand for Drugs*, Dublin: Stationery Office.

Ireland, Social Economy Working Group (1998), *Partnership 2000: Social Economy Working Group Report*, Dublin: Stationery Office.

Jaggar, A. (1989), "Love and Knowledge: emotion in feminist epistemology", in A. Jaggar and S. Bordo (eds.), *Gender/Body/Knowledge: Feminist Resolutions of Being and Knowing*, New Brunswick, New Jersey: Rutgers University Press.

Jolly, M. (1998), "Colonial and postcolonial plots in histories of maternities and modernities", In K. Ram and M. Jolly (eds.), *Maternities and Modernities: colonial and postcolonial experiences in Asia and the Pacific*, Cambridge: Cambridge University Press.

Kennedy, P. (1997), "A Comparative Study of Maternity Entitlements in Northern Ireland and the Republic of Ireland in the 1990s", in A. Byrne and M. Leonard (eds.), *Women and Irish Society: A Sociological Reader*, Belfast: Beyond the Pale Publications.

Kennedy, P. (1998), "Labouring Mothers: A Feminist Critique of Irish Social Policy", Ph.D. thesis, Department of Social Policy and Social Work, University College Dublin.

Keogh, E. (1997), *Illicit Drug Use and Related Criminal Activity in the Dublin Metropolitan Area*, Dublin: An Garda Síochána.

Leonard, M. (1997), "Women Caring and Sharing in Belfast", in A. Byrne and M. Leonard (eds.), *Women and Irish Society: A Sociological Reader*. Belfast: Beyond the Pale Publications.

Lingis, A. (1997), "Anger", in D. Shepherd et al. (eds.), *The Sense of Philosophy: On Jean-Luc Nancy*, London: Routledge.

Loughran, H. (1999), "Drugs Policies in Ireland in the 1990s", in S. Quin et al. (eds.), *Contemporary Irish Social Policy*, Dublin: UCD Press.

Lynch, K. (1998), "The Status of Children and Young Persons: Educational and Related Issues", in S. Healy and B. Reynolds (eds.), *Social Policy in Ireland: Principles, Practice and Problems*, Dublin: Oak Tree Press.

Lynch, K. (1999), "Equality Studies, the Academy and the Role of Research in Emancipatory Social Change", in *The Economic and Social Review*, Vol. 30, January, pp. 41–70.

Mayock, P. (2000), *Young people and drugs: the social experiences of young people in an inner-city community*, Dublin: Children's Centre, Trinity College Dublin.

McCann, M. (1998), "Drug services in Dublin: selective or comprehensive strategies", in *Journal of Substance Misuse*, 3, pp. 150–155.

McCarthy, D. (1999), *Evaluation of the ICON Drugs Support Services*, Dublin: ICON.

McCarthy, D. and McCarthy, P. (1997), *Dealing with the Nightmare: Drug Use and Intervention Strategies in South Inner City Dublin*, Dublin: Community Response.

McCashin, A. (1996), *Lone Mothers in Ireland: A Local Study*, Dublin: Combat Poverty Agency/Oak Tree Press.

McElrath, K. and McEvoy, K. (1999), *Ecstasy Use in Northern Ireland*, Belfast: HMSO.

McCoy, A. (1991), *The Politics of Heroin*, New York: Lawrence Hill Books.

Moran, R. (1999), "The availability, use and evaluation of the provision of crèche facilities in association with drug treatment", Dublin: Drug Misuse Research Division, Health Research Board.

Moran, R., O'Brien, M., and Duff, P. (1997), *Treated Drug Misuse in Ireland. National Report — 1996*, Dublin: Drug Misuse Research Division, Health Research Board.

Morgan, D.H.J. (1996), *Family Connections: An Introduction to Family Studies*, London: Polity Press.

Murphy, T. (1996), *Rethinking the War on Drugs in Ireland*, Cork: Cork University Press.

Murphy-Lawless, J. (1983), *The Community Service Project: Sean MacDermott Street*, Dublin: YEAG.

Murphy-Lawless, J. (2000), "Changing Women's Working Lives: Childcare Policy in Ireland", in *Feminist Economics*, Vol. 6, No. 1, March, pp. 89–94.

Murphy-Lawless, J. et al. (2000), *Problem Drug Use in Cabra*, Dublin: Finglas-Cabra Drugs Task Force.

National Drugs Strategy Unit (2001), *Building on Experience — National Drugs Strategy 2001–2008*, Department of Tourism, Sport and Recreation: NDSU.

NICDTF (2001), *Summary Strategy Plan 2001: Phase 2 of a programme for action*, Dublin: NICDTF.

Nolan, B. and Watson, D. (1999), *Women and Poverty in Ireland*, Dublin: Combat Poverty Agency/Oak Tree Press.

O'Brien, M. and Moran, R. (1997), *Overview of Drug Issues in Ireland*, Dublin: Health Research Board.

O'Connor, P. (1998), *Emerging Voices: Women in Contemporary Irish Society*, Dublin: IPA.

O'Gorman, A. (1999), *No Room for Complacency: Families, Communities and HIV*, Dublin: Cáirde.

O'Higgins, K. and Duff, P. (1997), *Treated Drug Misuse in Ireland: First National Report, 1995*, Dublin: Health Research Board.

O'Higgins, K. and O'Brien, M. (1994), *Treated Drug Misuse in the Greater Dublin Area: Report for 1992 and 1993*, Dublin: The Health Research Board.

O'Mahoney, P. (1993), *Crime and Punishment in Ireland*, Dublin: Round Hall.

O'Mahoney, P. (1998), "Punishing Poverty and Personal Adversity", in I. Bacik and M. O'Connell (eds.), *Crime and Poverty in Ireland*, Dublin: Round Hall, Sweet and Maxwell.

Reynolds, B. and Healy, S. (1994), *Towards an Adequate Income for All*, Dublin: CORI.

Rooney, E. (1997), "Women in Party Politics and Local Groups: Findings from Belfast", in A. Byrne and M. Leonard (eds.), *Women and Irish Society: A Sociological Reader*, Belfast: Beyond the Pale Publications.

Ross, E. (1995), "New Thoughts on the 'Oldest Vocation': Mothers and Motherhood in Recent Feminist Scholarship", in *Signs*, Vol. 20, No. 2, pp. 397–413.

Ruddick, S. (1989), *Maternal Thinking: Towards a Politics of Peace*, Boston: Beacon Press.

Ruddick, S. (1990), "Thinking about Fathers", in M. Hirsch and E. Fox Keller (eds.), *Conflicts in Feminism*, New York: Routledge.

Ruddick, S. (1993), "Maternal Thinking", in B.K. Rothman (ed.), *The Encyclopedia of Childbearing*, New York: Henry Holt.

Ruddle, H. et al. (2000), *Evaluation of Local Drugs Task Force Projects: Experiences and Perceptions of Planning and Implementation*, Dublin: Policy Research Centre, National College of Ireland.

Rush, M. (1997), "The Social Economy and Social Solidarity: Between the Market and the Public Sector", in Alliance for Work Forum (eds.), *Integrating the Social Economy Sector: New Services, New Jobs*, Dublin: Alliance for Work Forum.

Sabel, C. (1996), *Ireland: Local Partnerships and Social Innovation*, Paris: OECD.

Stack, C. (1996), "Writing Ethnography: Feminist Critical Practice", in D. Wolf (ed.), *Feminist Dilemmas in Fieldwork*, Boulder, CO: Westview Press.

Tronto, J. (1989), "Women and Caring: What Can Feminists Learn about Morality from Caring?" in A. Jaggar et al. (eds.), *Gender/Body/Knowledge: Feminist Knowledges of Being and Knowing*, New Brunswick: Rutgers University Press.

Varley, T. (1998), "More Power to the People? The Politics of Community Action in Late Twentieth-Century Ireland", in S. Healy and B. Reynolds (eds.), *Social Policy in Ireland: Principles, Practice and Problems*, Dublin: Oak Tree Press.

Wacquant, L. (1993), "Urban Outcasts: Stigma and Division in the Black American Ghetto and the French Urban Periphery", in *International Journal of Urban and Regional Research*, Vol. 17, No. 3, pp. 366–83.

Williams, A. (1990), *Reflections on the Making of an Ethnographic Text*, Studies in Sexual Politics, No. 29, Occasional papers, Manchester: Department of Sociology, University of Manchester.

YEAG (1983), "One factory for 8,000 people", press release, 21 April 1983.